WESTLAND
WESSEX

1958 onwards (all models)

COVER IMAGE: Westland Wessex HAS. Mk3.
(Mike Badrocke)

First published in April 2018
Reprinted July 2018

A catalogue record for this book is available from the British Library.

ISBN 978 1 78521 117 1

Library of Congress control no. 2017948771

Published by Haynes Publishing,
Sparkford, Yeovil,
Somerset BA22 7JJ, UK.
Tel: 01963 440635
Int. tel: +44 1963 440635
Website: www.haynes.com

Haynes North America Inc.,
859 Lawrence Drive, Newbury Park,
California 91320, USA.

Printed in Malaysia.

Senior Commissioning Editor: Jonathan Falconer
Copy editor: Michelle Tilling
Proof reader: Penny Housden
Indexer: Peter Nicholson
Page design: James Robertson

Acknowledgements

In producing this book, the author would like to extend his gratitude to the following individuals and organisations, without whose help and assistance it would not have been possible:

Leonardo Helicopters (formerly Westland Helicopters Ltd and AgustaWestland Ltd), in particular Mick Burrow, David Gibbings, Jerry Graham, Geoff Russell and Emily Weeks; David Ackroyd; David Barrow; David Baston; John Beattie; Peter Bell; Jeff Chartier; Pete Coley; Peter J. Cooper; Paul 'Dinkie' Davies; Ray Deacon; Gordon Douglas; Jonathan Falconer; David Gash; Steve George; Bob Girling; the staff of the Fleet Air Arm Museum, especially Barbara Gilbert and Catherine Cooper, Richard Barlow, Will Gibbs and David Morris; Richard Grevatte-Ball; the staff and volunteers of the International Helicopter Museum, especially Mark Service and Rod Holloway; Tony Jupp; Tammy Lee of HAECO; Danny Leeman; Mike Lehan; Derek Long; Pablo Martinez; Ian McGonagle; Pete Mesney; the late Eric Myall; Chris Page MBE; Sid Pass; David Paul; Graham Perry; Robin Perry; Peter Rawlings; Robbie Roberts; Andy Robinson of the Imperial War Museum Duxford; Anne McMillan and WO Nick Williams of RAF Shawbury; Tony Stafford; Ian Stanley DSO; Michelle Tilling of Bourchier Ltd; Bob Ward; Dave Wells; Pete Wendes; George White; Andrew Whitehouse; Nick Wiles; the late Dave Williams; Peter Wooldridge.

WESTLAND WESSEX

1958 onwards (all models)

Owners' Workshop Manual

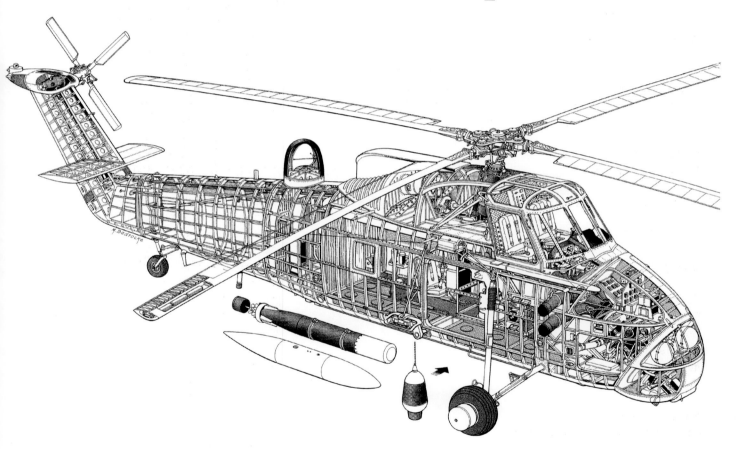

An insight into the design, construction, operation and maintenance of an anti-submarine, trooping, SAR and VVIP helicopter

Lee Howard

Contents

OPPOSITE Wessex HAR Mk.2 XT604 undergoing a check test flight after overhaul at the Helicopter Maintenance Flight based at RAF St Mawgan, Cornwall, before issue back to 22 Squadron 'C' Flight, RAF Valley, 4 October 1993. *(Peter J. Cooper)*

Introduction

'Flying Palm Tree', 'Walter', 'The Westland Fun Bus': the rugged, charismatic, versatile and much-loved Westland Wessex had an array of affectionate nicknames, serving with distinction with both the Royal Navy and the Royal Air Force for an incredible 44 years in operational theatres that ranged from Borneo through to the Falklands and Northern Ireland, as well as performing rotary-wing training and VIP communications transport roles.

Along with British military use, the Wessex was also operated by civilian companies for offshore freight and passenger services, as well as being the helicopter of choice for several foreign military air arms. Someone once summarised the early aircraft as being, '… a rattly, under-powered junk bucket by comparison to modern helicopters, but in its day it truly was "The Queen of the Skies"'.

All of the variants that saw operation with the British military – from the first HAS Mk.1s entering service with the Royal Navy in 1960, through the other Napier Gazelle-powered HAS Mk.3 and the Rolls-Royce Gnome-engined HC Mk.2, VVIP HCC Mk.4 and HU Mk.5 – as well as the Royal Australian Navy's HAS Mk.31 and HAS Mk.31B and the civil Mk.60 variant – are covered in this book. Although space precludes an exhaustive account of an aircraft with such a long, varied and illustrious career, the major notable events in its history from inception through to the type's eventual retirement with its last British military operator, the RAF, in 2003, are dealt with.

BELOW Cutaway of the Wessex HAS Mk.1. *(The Aeroplane)*

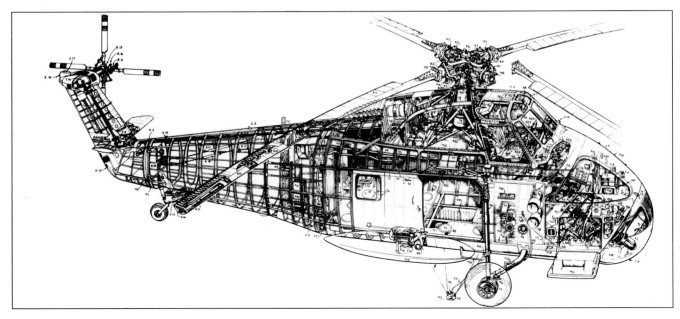

Several Wessex HU Mk.5s of 848 NAS, including XS483 ('E/A'), surrounded by drums of fuel at Nanga Gaat, Sarawak, in November 1965, during the Confrontation with Indonesia. *(Leonardo Helicopters)*

Chapter One

Helicopter developments

—●—

Although the helicopter had seen some military use in both Britain and America during the Second World War, its potential had never been fully exploited. America had led the way, carrying out the first recorded rescue operation by a Sikorsky YR-4 in Burma as early as April 1944, but the type was still very much under evaluation in Britain at the end of 1945. The Malayan Emergency of 1948–60 would end all of that and finally provide the first real opportunity to demonstrate the usefulness of the helicopter in modern warfare. But it was an altogether more peaceable role that it adopted first.

OPPOSITE Sikorsky HRS-2 Whirlwind HAR Mk.21 WV190 ('B') of 848 NAS demonstrating fast-roping as part of its anti-terrorist role in Malaya, 1955/56. *(Author's collection)*

In often inhospitable, inaccessible locations, the RAF had begun operating the Dragonfly HC.2s – military variants of Sikorsky S-51 helicopters built under a licence acquired by Westland Aircraft Ltd in 1947 – in the Far East with their CASEVAC Flight in support of Operation Firedog from May 1950. With special rescue 'litter' panniers fitted to the outside of the cabin in which single casualties could be carried either side, the aircraft could pick up wounded and sick soldiers and return them to base for urgent medical attention that would have otherwise often entailed days of trekking on foot through dense jungle.

Although managing to conduct the rescue of some 265 casualties during its three years of use, the Dragonfly was operating at the very limit of its capability. In the tropical heat and with one patient and one pilot, the aircraft could only carry enough fuel for 30 minutes of flying time, which equated to 30 miles' range.

Korean War 1950–52

While the RAF put their Dragonflies to use in Malaya, the US Marine Corps (USMC) was similarly putting their own Sikorsky HO3S-1 (military designation for the S-51) to use in rescuing downed pilots and carrying out casualty evacuation operations in Korea. These were also augmented by the US Air Force's (USAF) H-5 variants. Initially, the US Navy (USN) had loaned one of their helicopters to HMS *Theseus* before the Admiralty finally decided, in 1951, to withdraw its fixed-wing Supermarine Sea Otter aircraft from the plane-guard Air-Sea Rescue (ASR) role and replace them in the Light Fleet Carriers with British-built Westland Dragonflies. But as with the aircraft in Malaya, with their small cabins both the HO3S-1 and Dragonfly were hardly suited to lifting anything more than a crew of two.

Sikorsky's latest design, the HO4S-1 – the USN military variant of the new S-55 – would, however, soon prove to be a game-changer. Ordered in parallel by the USAF as the H-19 and by the USMC as the HRS-1, the aircraft featured a fully enclosed cabin separate from the cockpit which was perched high above the forward end.

Examples of the subsequent HRS-2 variant were also supplied to the Royal Navy as the trooping Whirlwind HAR Mk.21 and HO4S-3 as the anti-submarine Whirlwind HAS Mk.22 under the Mutual Defense Assistance Program. The HAR Mk.21s were quickly dispatched to Malaya with 848 Naval Air Squadron in 1953 where they became invaluable in moving troops and supplies around the jungles, quickly earning themselves the appellation 'Junglies' – a term that has endured to this day.

Westland Whirlwind

The Whirlwind became the second helicopter design acquired by Westland Aircraft Ltd from Sikorsky in the United States under the 1947 licence agreement. This had seen the company branch out from its traditional fixed-wing business into the rotary-wing world in building the military Dragonfly and civil WS-51, selling them throughout Europe and further afield.

The first WS-55 built by Westland Aircraft Ltd (it would not become Westland Helicopters Ltd until October 1965) had flown from its Yeovil factory on 12 November 1952 and became the Whirlwind HAR Mk.1 with the Royal Navy.

In taking the unusual step of abandoning the concept of nurturing in-house rotary-wing projects in favour of developing the mature designs of foreign companies, Westland had freed themselves from the difficult, time-consuming and expensive initial testing of the basic designs, funds for which the other helicopter-manufacturing firms in Britain at that time – Cierva, Fairey and Bristol – were fiercely competing against each other to win from the Ministry of Supply (MoS) in a bid to secure lucrative substantial military contracts.

The strategy had its risks, however. By taking this route, the company would immediately become ineligible for MoS funding. But the advantage that it did give them was a much more valuable head start over their rivals in developing reliable and viable helicopters. It was a strategy that would have far-reaching consequences. By leap-frogging the other rotary-wing manufacturers in being able to provide solutions to military helicopter requirements both quicker and cheaper than their rivals, the MoS eventually took the decision

to cancel the funding lines for indigenous British helicopter research and development altogether, instead opting to place more orders from Yeovil. In doing so, it precipitated the ultimate demise of the other three manufacturers whose helicopter assets would eventually be subsumed within the Westland portfolio as part of the mass rationalisation of the British aircraft industry in 1960.

The Westland-built Whirlwind was, however, much heavier than its American brethren. When the HAR Mk.2 variant of the RAF's 155 Squadron replaced the 848 NAS aircraft in Malaya towards the end of the campaign, it proved to have noticeably inferior performance and suffered from poor serviceability.

Sikorsky S-58

Meanwhile, across the Atlantic, the USN had already been looking towards the new generation of anti-submarine helicopters and had taken the bold step of choosing the Bell HSL-1 tandem-rotor helicopter to fulfil the requirement. Unlike single-rotor helicopters, those with a tandem rotor configuration are less susceptible to centre of gravity changes brought about by the positioning of heavy equipment, such as sonar gear, in the cabin. At the same time, the US Army opted for the new and impressively proportioned Sikorsky S-56 design for its heavy-lift transport role.

However, both types were beset by technical problems that ultimately led to their cancellation, which would have further ramifications across the Atlantic. While the US Army would go on to use the S-56 in Vietnam, with great irony the USN instead turned back to the design that Sikorsky had been working on in parallel to the S-56 as a fall-back option: the S-58.

Design work on the S-58 had begun as early as 1951. Effectively taking the S-55 fuselage design and fitting a S-56 tailcone with the original four wheels being replaced by a tricycle arrangement and a four-bladed rotor, the first production anti-submarine variant, the HSS-1N Seabat, made its first flight at Bridgeport on 20 September 1954. Examples began entering service with the USN in August 1955 with orders being placed that same year for the US Army (which designated it the H-34 Choctaw); the USMC followed suit two years later in 1957 with their own variant, the HUS-1 Seahorse, to be used in the utility and transport role.

Helicopter engines

While America blazed a trail in helicopter design and manufacture, early British post-war helicopter design and procurement was in stark contrast. Here, it was a story of frustration, muddled requirements and costly cancellations, all of which culminated in the decimation of a fledgling industry and the rise of Westland above

ABOVE The tandem-rotor Bell HSL-1 BuNo 129849 at NAS North Island, California, July 1956. The design was beset with many problems and an order for the Royal Navy was cancelled before any examples were delivered.
(via Tommy Thomason)

Promising an increase in power to weight ratio, however, was the gas turbine. But the output from the major engine manufacturers was still firmly directed by the MoS, which provided the necessary funding for the purchase and development of military equipment and which still regarded production for fighters, bombers and transport aircraft to be of a much higher priority.

Only an injection of government money to provide research and development capabilities would allow a gas turbine to be manufactured that was sufficiently small yet powerful enough to be considered for helicopter designs.

Cancellations

In 1956, the MoS cancelled all development work on the Anti-Submarine Bristol Type 191 tandem-rotor helicopter. The aircraft had been ordered by the MoS to equip the Fleet Air Arm for Anti-Submarine Warfare (ASW) duties. But, somewhat mirroring its American counterpart the HSL-1, and as with so many other helicopter designs of the time, the aircraft had undergone a tortuous gestation period and had suffered from various problems, notably significant transmission and vibration issues. Before any example actually flew, the funding was withdrawn and entire project shelved.

In a period already blighted by ill-conceived specifications and costly cancellations, it was a bitter blow to the fledgling industry which had placed much hope in the MoS ordering the type to invigorate organic British helicopter design and manufacturing capability. The helicopter had finally started to gain traction over its fixed-wing contemporaries as a viable mode of military transport, and securing the much-needed government funding that was constantly under threat in these times of post-war austerity was crucial to maintaining that position.

With an outstanding bill for £5 million, not only was the Type 191 a costly cancellation, but in 1957 it was compounded by the decision to withdraw the Royal Navy's Fairey Gannet ASW aircraft. This had led to the piston-engined Whirlwind assuming the role. The transfer of responsibility was, arguably, somewhat premature as the Alvis Leonides-powered HAS Mk.7 version would soon after

ABOVE Model of the cancelled Bristol Type 191 ASW tandem rotor helicopter whose development was also curtailed. *(Author's collection)*

all others to dominate the market with adapted American designs, aided by the emergence of the viable small gas turbine.

The issue of how to power helicopters would effectively come to define – and hold back – rotary-wing development in the early days. Throughout the late 1940s and early 1950s, piston engines were still the only form of power available to helicopter designers to drive the rotors. All of these were basic adaptations of engines fitted to existing fixed-wing aircraft, there being little in the way of civilian or military interest great enough to invest funds into the design and manufacture of a lightweight, yet powerful, alternative specifically for the helicopter. It was a constant trade-off between an engine's physical size, its weight and the power that it developed to overcome that weight and thus get the helicopter off the ground.

As the tasks expected of a helicopter became more varied, the requirement for greater engine power increased. This could only be provided by larger radial engines. But their bigger size was matched by their weight, which quickly negated any benefit that their increased power output might bring. This problem was made worse by the mass of additional fuel that the aircraft needed to carry, as well as a heavy clutch and cooling fan.

begin to experience significant engine problems, leading to many being lost. With the increase in Soviet submarine activity, losing anti-submarine helicopters with valuable sonar detection equipment on board was not acceptable. A more reliable, more capable alternative was needed. And quickly.

HAS.170D

In the wake of the Bristol 191 cancellation and ahead of more spending cuts, the MoS gave the go-ahead in April 1956 for a £3.5 million project to licence-build the Sikorsky S-58/HSS-1N Seabat in the UK. The Seabat had first flown at Sikorsky's Connecticut plant in March 1954, powered by a single Wright R-1820 radial piston engine.

Just four months after the cancellation of the Bristol 191, Specification HAS.170D was issued by the MoS against Naval Staff Requirement NA.43 Issue 4. Whereas specifications such as this were normally issued to competing companies which were then invited to tender their proposals, HAS.170D was effectively written around an Anglicised S-58 design, calling for an Anti-submarine and General Purpose helicopter fitted with a single gas turbine engine. Whereas each Type 191 had been expected to cost £140,000 each, the Anglicised S-58 was forecast to come in at just £103,000 each.

While the Royal Navy licked their wounds from the cancellation and the loss of the Gannets, they consoled themselves with the promise of an entirely different and largely already proven type of helicopter. The RAF, however, was still intent on proceeding with the development and procurement of the Bristol 192 – soon to become the Belvedere. Like the Type 191, the Belvedere was to be powered by two Napier Gazelle gas turbine engines.

BELOW Sikorsky HSS-1N 148957 'NT-59' of Helicopter Squadron 8 (HS-8) – 'The Eightballers' – preparing to 'dunk' its AN/AQS sonar in the western Pacific, 1962. *(via Nick Blackman)*

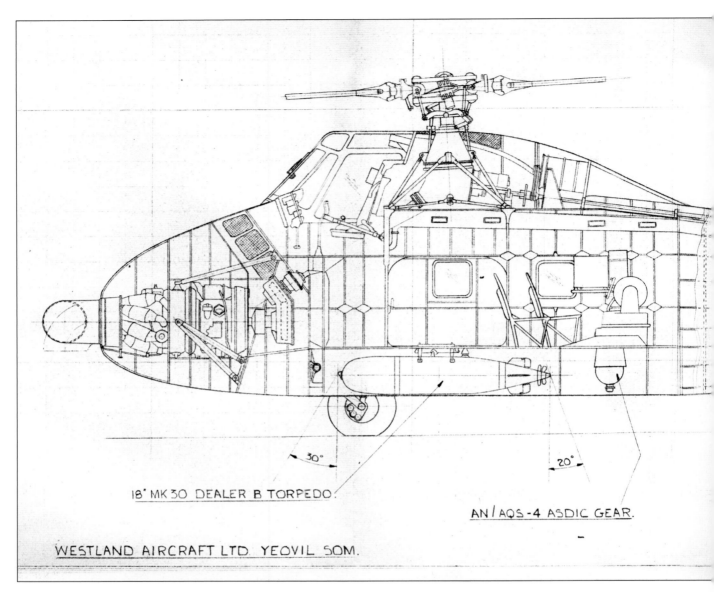

18" MK 30 DEALER B TORPEDO.

30°

20°

AN/AQS-4 ASDIC GEAR.

WESTLAND AIRCRAFT LTD. YEOVIL SOM.

The Gazelle was the first British gas turbine engine to have been designed from the outset for use in helicopters. Work had begun at Napier in 1954 and the first engine was run on 2 December 1955 with its subsequent development being funded by the MoS as part of the intended Bristol Type 191 and 192 programmes.

However, with only 26 Type 192s being ordered, conducting the necessary development work to bring such a reduced number of the new British engine into service and provide technical support throughout its life was deemed to be prohibitively expensive. Installing the Gazelle in the S-58 to replace its Wright Cyclone piston engine, and thereby necessitating an order much larger in number,

would, however, help to offset these costs. As a gas turbine engine powered by kerosene, it also brought with it the added attraction of negating the need to carry highly flammable AVGAS on board ships.

HSS-1N Seabat

In April 1956, Westland's Chief Test Pilot W.H. 'Slim' Sear travelled to Sikorsky's Connecticut factory to undertake a conversion course on the S-58. Here he flew HSS-1N Seabat 58265 which had originally been allocated to the USN as BuAer 141602 but which was now destined to be shipped to the UK for Westland to use as a trials aircraft.

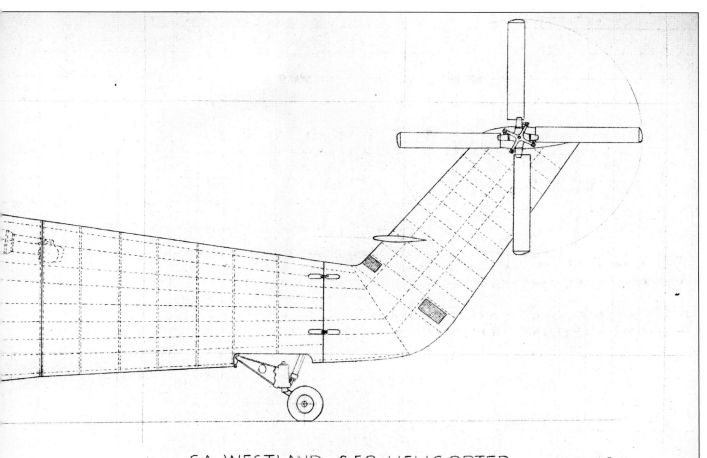

G.A. WESTLAND S.58. HELICOPTER. TO N.A.43.
SHOWING INSTALLATION OF DEALER B TORPEDO & AN/AQS-4 ASDIC GEAR.
SCALE - ½ INCH = 1 FOOT.

SECRET.

DRG.NO. PD.200.

1958

LEFT HSS-1N Seabat G-17-1 just prior to its first flight at Yeovil, still fitted with the original Wright Cyclone engine. Westland's last fixed-wing product, the Wyvern S.4, can be seen in the background.
(Leonardo Helicopters)

ABOVE Now registered as XL722, the Seabat was soon fitted with a Napier Gazelle engine featuring the first of several air intake designs. *(Leonardo Helicopters)*

Having accumulated 11 hours of flying time in the United States, the Seabat was dismantled and transported to Yeovil where, wearing Class B test flying registration marks G-17-1, it was test-flown by Sear on 24 June 1956. Still fitted with its original 1,525hp Wright R-1820-84 Cyclone, it would go on to complete some 76 hours of test flying. With the nose area subsequently modified to allow the fitting of a single 1,120shp Napier Gazelle NGa.11, Sear flew the aircraft, which on 10 July 1956 had been allocated the British military registration XL722, for just over an hour on 17 May 1957. Later still, a 1,450shp NGa.13 was installed featuring a modified 'eyelid' intake.

With the Gazelle being much smaller and

RIGHT The wooden mock-up of the Gazelle-powered Wessex taking shape in the Experimental Department at Yeovil, November 1956. *(Leonardo Helicopters)*

somewhat lighter than the Cyclone, and not requiring the usual heavy clutch and cooling fan assembly associated with piston engines fitted to helicopters, the aircraft was found to have a centre of gravity much further aft. A simple solution to correct this was to make use of the greater amount of free space above the engine and redesign the nose to incorporate equipment bays for the various radio and electrical equipment.

Following the success of the conversion of the Seabat, three pre-production HAS.170D prototypes were ordered by the Admiralty in May 1956. Looking much more representative of what would become the production aircraft, the first of these, XL727, first flew on 20 June

ABOVE A Wessex . . . of sorts. This ground training aid was manufactured to replicate all elements of the Wessex, including a folding tail. Built to teach successive generations of FAA engineers, it is still in use to this day. *(Leonardo Helicopters)*

RIGHT Westland Chief Test Pilot, W.H. 'Slim' Sear in front of XL722. *(Leonardo Helicopters)*

1958. This was followed shortly thereafter by XL728 and XL729.

Wessex

Finally, on 30 January 1959, the MoS formally announced that the HAS.170D naval variant would, following a company tradition of naming its aircraft beginning with the letter W, henceforth be known as the Westland Wessex. A legend had been born.

As well as these three Westland-built prototypes, a further nine pre-production aircraft – XM299 to XM301 and XM326 to XM331 – were ordered by the MoS in order to undertake the various engine, flight control system, handling and performance, cold and hot weather operations, sonar and carrier trials necessary to clear the aircraft for service use. All but the first three of these were later brought up to full production standard and went on to serve with front-line units.

By early 1960, the Wessex was finally ready to begin what would turn out to be nearly three decades of service with the Fleet Air Arm.

OPPOSITE The first of the pre-production aircraft, XM299, at Yeovil. This would later become the test-bed for the Gnome engine configuration. *(Leonardo Helicopters)*

Chapter Two

Royal Navy HAS Mk.1 and Mk.3

Although intended from the start as a pure anti-submarine helicopter, the Wessex HAS Mk.1 would quickly earn itself a reputation as being perhaps the most versatile of all of the British variants spanning a range of roles. From hunting submarines, it soon found itself being something of an aerial utility truck, moving troops and equipment in far-flung Borneo and later spearheading the type's use in Search and Rescue.

OPPOSITE Wessex HAS Mk.1 XS870 ('050/R') of 815 NAS, HMS *Ark Royal*, viewed from another Wessex cockpit during flying operations in the Far East, 1966. *(Tony Stafford)*

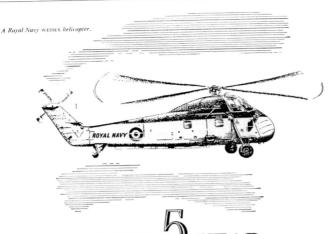

A Royal Navy WESSEX helicopter.

NEW 5 YEAR
COMMISSIONS AS HELICOPTER PILOTS
IN THE
ROYAL NAVY

IT WAS THE ROYAL NAVY which pioneered the Service use and operating techniques of helicopters.

Their versatility makes them of vital importance to the Navy for anti-submarine duties, landing Marine Commandos, rescue work and many other tasks.

You can now join as a commissioned officer for specialised training to serve as a helicopter pilot.

The term of engagement is five years and you will receive a tax-free gratuity of £675 on completion of service. The increasing use of helicopters offers opportunities to trained pilots in civil life afterwards. Ages of entry are between 17 and 23.

For full details, write to :

OFFICER ENTRY, Dept. FR/15, THE ADMIRALTY

QUEEN ANNE'S MANSIONS, LONDON, S.W.I.

Wessex HAS MK.1 – the 'Pingers'

The initial production order for the Wessex HAS Mk.1 was placed in February 1958 with the first aircraft, XM832, being delivered just over two years later in April 1960. By the time that the final aircraft emerged from the factory in 1966, some 128 Wessex HAS Mk.1s had been built at Yeovil.

But despite being intended for use against the perceived Soviet submarine threat in NATO waters, it would be the British withdrawal from its overseas commitments east of Suez that would end up being the aircraft's main theatre of operation throughout most of the 1960s.

700H NAS

The HAS Mk.1 would eventually equip 12 Naval Air Squadrons (NAS) and various Flights for nearly two decades. The first example

ABOVE A contemporary FAA recruitment advert featuring the original Seabat XL722. (Author's collection)

RIGHT Wessex HAS Mk.1 XM839 ('512') of 700H NAS at RNAS Culdrose. The aircraft is fitted with a tie-down brace around the tail. (Noel Collier)

RIGHT **Wessex HAS Mk.1 XS886 ('(5)73/CU')**
of 706 NAS while on loan to HMS Eagle. Note
the temporary code numbers applied in black
masking tape. *(Geoff Wakeham)*

entered British military service with 700H NAS
at RNAS Culdrose on 1 April 1960 where it
was evaluated in the anti-submarine search
and strike role. All aspects of the engine and
airframe, autopilot and weapons systems were
put through their paces ahead of the aircraft
entering front-line use with the Fleet Air Arm.

706 NAS

The aircraft of 700H NAS were immediately
re-formed as 706 NAS to undertake the role
of the Advanced Flying Training squadron,
providing specialist operational training to
helicopter pilots before they moved on to the
front-line units as well as undertaking trials work.

815 NAS

The first front-line unit to receive the Wessex
was 815 NAS on 4 July 1961. Within weeks of

RIGHT **815 NAS personnel spreading the main**
rotor blades of Wessex HAS Mk.1 XM843 ('301/R')
using HMS Ark Royal's semi-lowered deck lift to
bring the blade tips within reach of those on the
deck. *(David Dawson-Taylor)*

LEFT **A Wessex**
pilot's view of Fairey
Gannet AEW Mk.3
landing on HMS Ark
Royal while another
815 NAS Wessex HAS
Mk.1, XS863 ('054/R'),
conducts plane-guard
duties in 1966.
(Tony Stafford)

leaving for the Mediterranean, however, engine problems led to the aircraft being shipped back to the UK for urgent modification action before rejoining the ship early in the new year.

819 NAS

Re-formed out of 719 NAS at RNAS Eglinton, Northern Ireland, in October 1961, 819 NAS became the Wessex HQ Squadron, teaching ASW techniques in conjunction with the Joint Anti-Submarine School at nearby Londonderry. Equipped with the HAS Mk.1, these were eventually replaced by the HAS Mk.3 in April 1968.

814 NAS

In November 1961, 814 NAS re-formed at Culdrose for service aboard HMS *Hermes* in the Mediterranean. A year later the squadron sailed with the ship to the Far East before transferring to HMS *Victorious*. In 1964, the aircraft saw action in Borneo where they briefly assisted their 'Junglie' brethren during the Indonesian Confrontation.

ABOVE Wessex HAS Mk.1 XM872 ('320/H') of 819 NAS, based at RAF Ballykelly. The aircraft wears a 'Red Hand of Ulster' over the deck letter 'H' and is fitted with the early type of flotation canister on the main undercarriage. *(Author's collection)*

BELOW Wessex HAS Mk.1 XP147 ('270/V') and two others of 814 NAS approaching the deck of HMS *Victorious* in the Indian Ocean, 1963. Note that the aircraft have amber screens fitted to their windows for night flying operations. *(Author's collection)*

LEFT Wessex HAS Mk.1 XP157 ('405/LO') of 737 NAS HMS *London* Flight was the last Ship's Flight Mk.1 to see service, seen here at RNAS Lee-on-Solent on 28 June 1972. *(A.W.M. Groth)*

CENTRE Wessex HAS Mk.1 XS122 ('290/E') of 820 NAS on plane guard duties alongside HMS *Eagle*. *(Author's collection)*

737 NAS

Receiving its first Wessex HAS Mk.1s in July 1962 with HAS Mk.3s joining in March 1967, 737 NAS conducted all training on type before the crews were sent to their respective front-line squadrons or Flights. The responsibility for parenting all Wessex embarked in the eight County-class destroyers was passed from 829 NAS to 737 NAS at Portland in June 1970. The last of the squadron's HAS Mk.1s, that of HMS *London* Flight, was finally retired in May 1978.

829 NAS

In March 1964, 829 NAS re-formed at Culdrose where it became responsible as the headquarters unit for all Wasp and Wessex helicopters embarked in frigates and County-class destroyers.

820 NAS

Re-formed at Culdrose in September 1964, 820 NAS operated Wessex HAS Mk.1s from the aircraft carrier HMS *Eagle* in the ASW role and replaced them with the HAS Mk.3 from May 1969.

826 NAS

The last of the HAS Mk.1 squadrons to form was 826 NAS at Culdrose in March 1966, operating the type in the ASW role until being replaced by HAS Mk.3s in October 1968. Two examples were retained as dedicated Search and Rescue (SAR) aircraft with the squadron until disbandment in March 1970.

Aden 1963–67

Located at the southernmost part of the Red Sea and guarding the route to and from the

LEFT Wessex HAS Mk.1s XS881 ('344/H') and XS886 ('346/H') of 826 NAS. *(Tony Stafford)*

Suez Canal, Aden was naturally of strategic importance to Britain and its need to maintain sea links with its empire east of Suez.

Following the Suez Crisis of 1956, however, a wave of Arab nationalism had swept through the Middle East and, in October 1963, an anti-British uprising began in Aden which triggered a state of emergency that was to precipitate the ultimate handover of the colony four years later.

With fighting having broken out between local tribesmen and the invading Army of the Federation of South Arabian States in the mountainous Radfan area close to the border with Yemen in January 1964, British land forces were deployed to drive out rebels who had earlier crossed the border into Yemen where they had been trained, armed and subsequently returned to Aden to continue the fight.

As the intensity of violence increased, 815 NAS were quickly embarked in HMS *Centaur* at Singapore during May and set a westerly course bound for Aden. En route, their anti-submarine Wessex HAS Mk.1s were quickly re-roled, being stripped of their sonar equipment and superfluous items such as cabin heaters to reduce weight. To make them more suitable to trooping and freight-carrying, makeshift cabin floor protection consisting of coconut matting covered with canvas was fitted to all aircraft and, on some, Bren gun mountings installed in the doorway.

Having disembarked from the ship to RAF Khormaksar on arrival soon after, the squadron found that there was little in the way of suitable support infrastructure for helicopters. Some Wessex had to have tie-down ground runs conducted by lashing the front end of the aircraft to a tie-down base designed for a Whirlwind while hanging all of the available crane testing weights that could be found on the air station over the tail.

With a forward operating base (FOB) being established at Thumier airstrip some 45 miles north of Khormaksar, the Wessex were immediately put to use in 'leapfrogging' supplies, equipment and replacement troops by air to ground forces as the dissidents were gradually pushed back through the Wadi territories. All the while, supporting air cover

and ground attacks against the rebels was provided by RAF Hunters operating from Khormaksar.

The weather in the Radfan area was notoriously unpredictable and challenging. Temperatures, even several thousand feet up, could often exceed 30°C with strong, turbulent winds. Torrential rains descended upon the barren land with little or no forewarning, with walls of water often meeting Army convoys half way up a mountain, sweeping them away and leaving many vehicles submerged. One 815 NAS Wessex pilot noted at the time, 'There cannot be many anti-submarine [helicopter] crews who have done a live SAR mission from a Saracen [armoured personnel carrier], 2,000ft up in the desert!'

ABOVE Wessex HAS Mk.1 XM889 ('305/C') of 815 NAS operating from HMS *Centaur* in Aden. The aircraft's ASW equipment has been stripped out to make it more capable for troop transportation. *(Author's collection)*

RIGHT The curse
of the Gazelle
engine strikes again!
Bedraggled and bent
Wessex HAS Mk.1
XS121 ('295/E') of 820
NAS is winched back
aboard HMS *Eagle*
after ditching,
25 March 1965.
(via Theo Ballance)

With the heat and altitude combination sapping the Wessex's single Gazelle engine of power, lifting heavy loads posed a problem. This was solved by operating at bare minimum fuel levels to keep the aircraft's weight down and conducting frequent rotors-running refuels in between lifts, with crews changed after two hours.

After completing some 124 sorties in Aden, 815 NAS left in HMS *Centaur* for Tanganyika to quell a mutiny before the Wessex returned once again to Aden in May and then, via Singapore, to the UK where 815 NAS disbanded once more at the end of the year.

Engine problems

Despite the promise of much greater performance that re-engining the S-58 design with a gas turbine would bring, if an aircraft could ever be said to have had an Achilles heel, then for the Wessex HAS Mk.1 it ironically came in the form of its single Napier Gazelle engine.

Throughout its life, it was beset by a number of catastrophic fatigue failures of mechanical items including reduction gearbox sun, planet and annulus gearing, oil tubes, compressors and quill shafts. Bangs, whines, loud metallic grinding noises and vibrations were all too often experienced, usually followed in quick succession by the spectacle of sparks and long sheets of flame emanating from the exhausts, and shortly thereafter by turbine blades departing through the engine casing. Invariably these would come up through the engine bay and cockpit, severing fuel lines and puncturing the fuel tank as they made their exit, leading to intense kerosene-fed fires and explosions.

Between 1961 and 1966, an astonishing 26 Wessex HAS Mk.1s were destroyed through such faults, 18 of which were attributed to the reduction gearbox. These failures often occurred when the engine reached a particular number of flying hours. As these time limits approached, many aircrew were – perhaps not irrationally – said to suddenly develop a reluctance to fly, lest they became yet another statistic. It was only in 1965 that the numbers of aircraft totally lost began to reduce, not by virtue of any change to the engine, but owing to the introduction of flotation gear which allowed the aircraft to float and be recovered following an engine failure-induced ditching.

The 'Junglie' Mk.1s – Borneo

In January 1963, Indonesia declared a policy of Confrontation in opposition to the British proposal to amalgamate the Federation of Malaya, Singapore and the British protectorates of North Borneo and Sarawak under the new name of Malaysia. This plan was a precursor to Britain's phased withdrawal from South-East Asia following the declaration of independence by Malaya and Singapore and the division, in 1961, of the island of Borneo into Kalimantan, the Sultanate of Brunei, British Borneo (Sabah) and Sarawak. Indonesia, supported by the Soviet Union, had been making great claims over territory in the Far East and the spread of communism throughout the region was becoming an increasing threat.

An Indonesian-inspired revolt in Brunei intended to preclude their joining in the Federation in December 1962 had quickly been quelled by British forces assisted by Whirlwinds of 846 NAS, demonstrating yet again the

ABOVE Wessex HAS Mk.1 XP103 ('W/B') of 845 NAS in the Light Stone paint finish being refuelled by locals employed to help support the aircraft at Nanga Gaat. *(Leonardo Helicopters)*

LEFT Wessex HAS Mk.1 of 845 NAS delivering supplies to a remote landing site in Borneo. Note the abundance of discarded empty fuel drums. *(Author's collection)*

value of helicopters. But, despite increasing opposition, the Federation of Malaysia formally came into being on 28 September 1963.

Wessex HAS Mk.1 utility

The standard Wessex HAS Mk.1 that equipped the Junglie units differed essentially in having all of the ASW equipment in the cabin removed and basic 'rag and tube'-type seating installed. Provision was also made for the carriage of stretchers for CASEVAC missions.

845 NAS

Embarking its mixed complement of utility-configured Wessex HAS Mk.1, Whirlwind HAS Mk.7 and Hiller HT.2 aircraft in the Commando carrier HMS *Bulwark* in March 1964, 706B NAS was absorbed into the front line as 845 NAS en route to Borneo. Wessex, Whirlwind and one Hiller were deployed ashore to Sarawak to set

ABOVE 845 NAS Wessex HAS Mk.1s, now with green camouflage applied over the Light Stone finish, lined up on HMS *Bulwark*. *(Colin Hague)*

BELOW Aircrew had the unenviable task of operating a single-engined Wessex HAS Mk.1 over dense primary jungle with few places to land. *(Colin Hague)*

Further east from Nanga Gaat through the Hose Mountains was Long Jawi, the scene of an early incursion by a large force of regular Indonesian Army troops against a handful of Gurkhas and Border Scouts. An ensuing massacre of the defenders did not warm the local Ibans to the Indonesian cause.

Long Jawi, a 40-minute flight from the Gaat, was subsequently defended by a company of the Royal Malay Regiment. It often saw frenzied activity when air drops of fuel and rations were made on the nearby dropping zone; the small missionary airstrip on the opposite bank was too small and adjacent to the Balui river for the Valettas and Hastings to land or use as a drop zone (DZ). 50-gallon fuel drums were heli-lifted into a central location for squadron use while palletised stores drops were split and sorted into separate loads for onward transportation to the four-man Special Forces (SF) patrols of such units as the Special Air Service (SAS), Royal Marines, Paras and Gurkhas. Aviation fuel which could not be used because of possible water contamination was made available to the local villagers for their paraffin lamps; they, in turn, often reciprocated with strings of beads – a bizarre turnaround from the days of the Raj!

SF patrols operated along the border area which was generally unpopulated but in the far north-east of the Division a tribe of Punans were discovered who lived in a village called Punan Busang. The Punans didn't respect any border demarcation and operated freely across it and were, therefore, a precious source of intelligence and local knowledge. A patrol based near the village was encouraged to integrate with the local populace and gain their trust. The location was somewhat remote and required an hour and a half's flying from Long Jawi. In a single-engine Wessex Mk.1 without modern navigation aids this was accomplished using maps singularly devoid of features in the time-honoured tradition of dead reckoning. The Topos of 84 Survey Squadron, Royal Engineers were busy trying to map and fill in the great blank spaces; Bukit Robertson, a 5,609ft peak named after a squadron pilot who died flying from Nanga Gaat, is testimony to 845's involvement. A group of 20 Royal Military Policemen (RMPs) were airlifted to a mosquito-infested riverbank for a three-week stay to develop a landing site en route; clearly someone 'on high' had a sense of humour or worse! Today, we might call it adventure training or character-building.

It should be noted that the Punans of this village had never seen a road or railway and lived an isolated existence, but they soon became accustomed to the Wessex helicopters making irregular visits to their community. Landings were made in a clearing close to the village huts which were fragile single-room structures made of branches and tree ferns. Often a toucan or a monkey could be seen on a perch by a flap doorway next to a row of blowpipes. Structures were not substantial as the village would be moved en masse a few hundred yards away whenever a death occurred.

BELOW David Ackroyd with a Wessex HAS Mk.1 of 845 NAS.
(David Ackroyd)

up their main operating base at the civil airport at Sibu in support of the 2nd Division (West) and a forward operating base further east at Nanga Gaat to support the 3rd Division (East), covering an area roughly the size of Scotland.

Nanga Gaat, the site of a former saw mill, was situated at the confluence of the rivers Gaat and Baleh. Trees had been cut down by Gurkha engineers to provide landing spots for the helicopters and personnel were accommodated by the Army in traditional atap-type 'bashas' built from bamboo. 'The Gaat', as it became known, even had its own pub – the Anchor Inn.

Because of its location deep within the jungle, drums of aviation fuel and other essential supplies had to be ferried in long boats 35 miles up the river from Kapit. Forward refuelling bases were also set up at Belaga and Long Jawi to cover the flying task.

The Wessex were expected to be capable of carrying up to eight troops, plus kit (200lb each) and 11,800lb of fuel from locations in temperatures normally between 30 and 34°C and with less than 5 knots of wind.

The hazardous nature of jungle operations led to some challenging flying and engineering activity. On one occasion a Wessex had to make an emergency landing on the only piece of available ground not covered by trees: a shingle bank in the middle of the River Baleh. These were often used as impromptu landing sites but

ABOVE A Wessex HAS Mk.1 nestled within a landing site clearing cut by Gurkha engineers. Some of the trees in Borneo could well exceed 200ft in height.
(Author's collection)

RIGHT Wessex HAS Mk.1s of 845 NAS and a solitary Whirlwind HAS Mk.7 of 846 NAS at Nanga Gaat. Stockpiles of fuel drums can be seen alongside the primitive accommodation.
(Author's collection)

only for short periods, not for emergencies. With the river having been known to rise as much as 12ft in as many hours, the maintainers managed to change the engine in just five hours. Shortly after the aircraft had flown out, the bank was swallowed up by the rising waters and was not seen again for over a month.

In 1964, the Wessex of 845 NAS began highly secretive Operation Claret missions which saw British SF being flown in to strategic jungle locations from where they would make limited incursions across the border into Indonesian Kalimantan to seek out and monitor dissident groups intent on mounting attacks. This information was then relayed to infantry units who would pursue a policy of keeping one step ahead of the Indonesians and forcing them to remain on a defensive rather than an offensive footing.

No. 845 NAS and their Wessex HAS Mk.1s were eventually relieved by 848 NAS in 1965 who brought with them new Wessex HU Mk.5s in HMS *Albion*.

Search and Rescue Mk.1s

As the Whirlwind began to be withdrawn from carrier service, so the responsibility for provision of SAR coverage gradually passed to whatever anti-submarine Wessex-equipped squadron was embarked at the time. Aircraft would be specifically allocated for the duty with relevant role equipment removed from the cabin to make them more compatible.

With the introduction of the Wessex HAS Mk.3, however, the increased complexity of the integrated anti-submarine equipment meant that changing the role of the aircraft became impossible. As a result, from late 1967 the fixed-wing carriers – HMS *Ark Royal*, HMS *Eagle*, HMS *Hermes* and HMS *Victorious* –

RIGHT **HMS *Eagle* SAR Flight Wessex HAS Mk.1 XM845 ('146/E') on the flight deck lift being brought up from the hangar.** *(George Gray)*

LEFT In rough weather conditions, the winch operator in the cabin doorway of Wessex HAS Mk.1 XM874 ('519/PO') of RNAS Portland-based 771 NAS lowers the diver to a 'survivor' in the English Channel. *(Author's collection)*

began to receive their own dedicated Ship's SAR Flight Wessex HAS Mk.1s fitted out for SAR operations. RNAS Yeovilton also had its own SAR Wessex operated by the Station Flight from December 1970.

771 and 772 NAS

The Whirlwind HAS Mk.7s of 771 NAS at RNAS Portland began to be replaced by Wessex HAS Mk.1s from November 1969. The unit moved to RNAS Culdrose in September 1974 but left six aircraft behind at Portland which became the newly re-formed 772 NAS. These aircraft provided SAR coverage along the south coast as well as support to RN and foreign military ships operating in the area and took part in national security exercises. No. 772 NAS replaced the HAS Mk.1s with HU Mk.5s in 1976.

Meanwhile, at Culdrose, 771 NAS joined the RN Flying Training School, responsible for training aircrewmen as well as providing SAR coverage around the south-west.

In 1974, the Royal Navy's shore-based SAR units finally bade farewell to the Wessex HAS Mk.1 and were re-equipped with HU Mk.5s specially fitted out for the task. The last of the carrier-borne SAR Wessex was retired when HMS *Ark Royal* was decommissioned in 1978, leaving 771 NAS as the final operator until they too were replaced by HU Mk.5s in 1979.

Wessex HAS Mk.3

By 1958, with the impending withdrawal of the Fairey Gannet fixed-wing aircraft from the anti-submarine role against the backdrop of increased submarine activities from behind the Iron Curtain, the focus on the use of helicopters in the ASW role became even more intense.

LEFT Not all rescues were of the human variety. Here, a Wessex HAS Mk.1 of 771 NAS from RNAS Culdrose lifts a stranded cow from the Cornish coastline to safety. *(RNAS Culdrose)*

ABOVE A meticulous line-up of retired Wessex HAS Mk.1s outside the Air Engineering School, RNAS Lee-on-Solent, during the 1980s. *(A.W.M. Groth)*

In May 1960, as the Wessex HAS Mk.1 was starting to roll off the production line, a Westland design study was published which looked at the provision of an improved ASW variant, specifically to allow it to carry the improved Type 195 Asdic dipping sonar. Written against Specification HAS.211T, the aircraft would also be equipped with two Mk.44 torpedoes, Blue Orchid Doppler, positional lightweight radar and a plotting system.

Adding this extra equipment and improving capability, of course, brought with it an increase in weight, initially estimated at some 725lb, all of which would drastically reduce the aircraft's endurance from the NATO requirement of 2 hours to just 1 hour 15 minutes. To offset this, options were put forward to re-engine the existing Wessex HAS Mk.1. Typical of the time, where investment in British engineering was encouraged over arguably better and more cost-effective foreign alternatives, a restriction was placed on the choice of engine to being 'any suitable gas turbine or turbines of British Manufacture'. The subsequent proposals were for either a single, developed Gazelle or a pair of Gnomes coupled to a common gearbox. Such an aircraft, it was predicted, would be available by mid-1963.

With design and development work by now heavily committed to the production of the RAF's new HC Mk.2, the decision was taken to go for the former option and install a Gazelle NGa.18 Mk.165 engine instead of the coupled Gnomes in what was always acknowledged to be a stop-gap variant pending the introduction of the proposed replacement ASW aircraft by 1970 (eventually emerging as the Westland Sea King).

In 1963, Westland received the official Instruction to Proceed from the Ministry of Aviation with the conversion of 43 existing Wessex HAS Mk.1 aircraft into the improved Wessex to be designated the HAS Mk.3, all of which was undertaken at Yeovil between 1965 and 1968.

BELOW Wessex HAS Mk.3 XM328 ('653/PO') of 737 NAS preparing to conduct a night training sortie for observers at RNAS Portland. *(via Nick Blackman)*

RIGHT 'Bootsie'! To prevent the loss of the new sonar equipment when conducting development trials over the water, Wessex HAS Mk.3 XM331 was fitted with inflatable pontoons shortly after conversion at Yeovil in 1968. *(Leonardo Helicopters)*

700H NAS

No. 700H NAS re-formed again as the Wessex HAS Mk.3 Intensive Flying Trials Unit formed once more at RNAS Culdrose on 9 January 1967 and quickly earned the unkind nickname 'The Culdrose Camel Corps', owing to the aircraft's distinctive radome 'hump' outline. One aircraft had been fitted with large inflatable pontoons for the duration of the Type 195 sonar trials in Portland Harbour, fitted in case the aircraft ditched to allow it to float and thus save the valuable detection equipment from being lost. Inevitably this particular aircraft became affectionately known as 'Bootsie'.

706 NAS

In July 1967, Wessex HAS Mk.3s began to arrive with 706 NAS, operating alongside the HAS Mk.1s before both were withdrawn in 1971.

BELOW No. 706 NAS Wessex HAS Mk.3 XM872 ('569/CU') flying over the Cornish coastline. *(via Geoff Wakeham)*

814 NAS

In October 1967, 814 NAS re-equipped with the HAS Mk.3, initially operating from Royal Fleet Auxiliary ships before embarking once again in HMS *Hermes* for passage to the Far East and Australia. The Wessex were finally relinquished when the squadron disbanded in July 1970.

826 NAS

No. 826 NAS replaced all but two of its HAS Mk.1 aircraft with HAS Mk.3s in October 1968, operating from HMS *Hermes*. All of the aircraft were retired when the squadron decommissioned in March 1970.

737 NAS

The Wessex HAS Mk.3 joined the Wessex HAS Mk.1s in 737 NAS in March 1967. During 1973 and, later, between 1975 and 1976, aircraft embarked in Royal Fleet Auxiliary (RFA) ships

WESSEX HAS MK.3 PROTOTYPES

XT255–XT257

WESSEX HAS MK.3 CONVERSIONS

XM327; XM328; XM331; XM833; XM834; XM836; XM837; XM838; XM844; XM870; XM871; XM872; XM916; XM919; XM923; XM927; XP104; XP105; XP110; XP116; XP118; XP137; XP138; XP139; XP140; XP142; XP143; XP147; XP150; XP153; XP156; XS121; XS122; XS126; XS127; XS149; XS153; XS862.

XP142

Undoubtedly the most famous of all of the Gazelle-powered Wessex is XP142, known to most as 'Humphrey'. Originally built as an HAS Mk.1 in June 1962, XP142 saw service with 845 NAS in Borneo during the Indonesian Confrontation where she was adorned with the cartoon character 'Mr Jinx' on the nose. Returning to the UK, she was operated with 706 NAS at Culdrose before being converted to HAS Mk.3 standard at Yeovil in 1969.

Thereafter, XP142 flew with 814 NAS, 706 NAS once again and then joined 737 NAS, operating with 106 Flight aboard the County-class destroyers HMS *Fife* and HMS *Hampshire* before joining 100 Flight in HMS *Antrim* where she was nicknamed 'Humphrey'.

On 25 April 1982, Humphrey located with its radar and then attacked and disabled the Argentinian submarine *Santa Fe* by straddling it with a pair of Mk.11 depth charges. This was the first time since the end of the Second World War – and, to date, the only time – that an enemy submarine has been successfully intercepted with live weapons.

Having returned from the South Atlantic, Humphrey was retired to the Fleet Air Arm Museum at RNAS Yeovilton, where she resides to this day.

were used during the 'Cod Wars' with Iceland, wearing the blue and yellow fishery protection pennants on the fuselage.

In 1974, a Wessex HAS Mk.3 of 737 NAS HMS *Devonshire* was involved in the rescue of British nationals from Northern Cyprus following the Turkish invasion with some 73 people eventually being transferred, crammed in the rear cabin around the sonar equipment, to safety.

The retirement of the last of the HAS Mk.3s was delayed when both HMS *Antrim* and HMS *Glamorgan* were sent to the South Atlantic with the Task Force to help retake the Falkland Islands, eventually being relinquished in December 1982.

RIGHT Wessex HAS Mk.3 XS862 ('406/ AN') securely lashed to the confined flight deck of HMS *Antrim* while disembarking passengers from Torishima, 5 May 1973. *(David Parry)*

ABOVE A Wessex HAS Mk.3 of 737 NAS 'burning and turning' on the flight deck of the County-class destroyer HMS *Devonshire*. *(Author's collection)*

LEFT Wessex HAS Mk.3 XM923 at RNAY Fleetlands painted in Olive Drab for special operations in Northern Ireland with 737 NAS 102/HMS *London* Flight. *(Author's collection)*

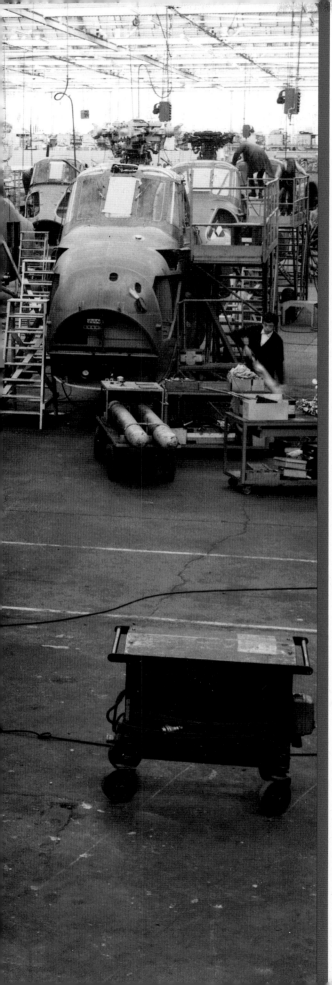

Chapter Three

Royal Air Force HC Mk.2

In comparison with the Royal Navy, the Royal Air Force had been relatively slow to accept rotary-wing aircraft as a valuable and viable mode of transport. Use of the Westland Dragonflies in 1950 for casualty evacuation duties during the Malayan Emergency, and later with the Whirlwind to assist the Army with trooping movements around the jungle, would change perceptions forever and secure the helicopter's place in modern warfare.

OPPOSITE Engineers push and shove the port Gnome engine into place in the nose of one of several brand new Wessex under construction in the Erecting Shop at Yeovil.
(Leonardo Helicopters)

In January 1960, Westland announced a further, £0.7million development of the Wessex: the HC (Helicopter Cargo) Mk.2. Although the aircraft was to equip the RAF, its purpose was to support the British Army's short-range helicopter requirement to get small detachments of soldiers as near as possible to the frontline in areas where the terrain was difficult or there was special urgency.

Replacing the single Napier Gazelle engine were two de Havilland (later to become Bristol Siddeley and ultimately Rolls-Royce) Gnome H.1000 gas turbine powerplants arranged in a coupled configuration to a common gearbox to improve the 'hot and high' performance. On the production aircraft these were soon replaced by more powerful H.1200 variants.

With the cancellation of the Bristol 191 project, and with only a small number of Belvederes available in the Short-Range Transport role, the RAF was keen to plug the gap and placed their first order in August the following year. HAS Mk.1 development aircraft, XM299, was given a 'nose job', substantially redesigning the forward structure in front of the cockpit to allow the two Gnomes and coupling gearbox to be installed. In this configuration, the aircraft flew for the first time at Yeovil on

ABOVE De Havilland Engines engineers working on the original coupled and inclined Gnome H.1000 and coupling gearbox test rig devised for the Wessex HC Mk.2 programme.
(de Havilland)

RIGHT 'Slim' Sear (centre) posing at Yeovil with Wessex HAS Mk.1 pre-production aircraft XM299, which had been converted to become the Gnome flying test-bed aircraft.
(Leonardo Helicopters)

18 January 1962 in the hands of 'Slim' Sear. Although intended as a variant for the RAF, the aircraft incongruously still bore its previous 'Royal Navy' markings.

By now, production had already begun and, on 15 October 1962, Sear flew the first of the RAF's aircraft, XR588. Resplendent in green/grey camouflage with aluminium-painted undersides, it immediately began manufacturer's trials at Yeovil.

Squadron service

The Wessex Intensive Flying Trials Unit (IFTU) was formed on 1 July 1963 at RAF Odiham, Hampshire, with the first of four aircraft being delivered there on 9 August to gain experience on the type and conduct intensive flying trials. Despite engine-related issues and one aircraft, XR500, being badly damaged on landing at Ternhill on 12 September, aircraft utilisation was found to be twice that which had been experienced with the Belvedere and

Folland Gnat trainer IFTUs. The trials officially ended on 26 January the following year.

18 Squadron

The concept of helicopters being used in support of British Army of the Rhine (BAOR) units protecting NATO's eastern flank in West Germany against the prospect of Soviet attack had only been adopted by the RAF following the success of Exercise Blind Mouse 4 in July 1962. Whirlwinds and Belvederes from Odiham

were detached to Gütersloh and, from January 1963, 230 Squadron were duly deployed to Gütersloh in support of 1 (British) Corps.

The first frontline unit to receive the Wessex HC Mk.2 was 18 Squadron, re-formed under No. 38 Group of RAF Transport Command at Odiham in January 1964 with 15 aircraft. The training role, which was initially provided by the squadron's own Wessex Conversion Flight, was transferred to 72 Squadron that November ahead of 18 Squadron moving to Gütersloh in January 1965 to relieve 230 Squadron.

The squadron returned to the UK in January 1968, basing itself at RAF Acklington, Northumberland. The stay was to be short, however, as it returned to RAF Odiham in July 1969.

In August 1970, 18 Squadron moved once again to Germany with its main operating base at RAF Gütersloh, while four aircraft of 'C' Flight were detached to RAF Wildenrath to provide support for the Harrier fixed-wing squadrons based there.

Each year, the squadron was given an opportunity to prove its ability to provide helicopter support to 1 (BR) Corps during Exercise Peg-Out. The Wessex would be spread out in hides in woods, heavily camouflaged to prevent detection from the air.

In December 1980, the Wessex finally left West Germany, being replaced on the squadron by Chinooks on return to the UK and in Germany by the Puma HC Mk.1s of 230 Squadron.

Cyprus detachments

At the same time that 18 Squadron moved to Germany, three of the squadron's aircraft were shipped to RAF Nicosia to replace 230 Squadron's Whirlwinds in the United Nations Peacekeeping Force in Cyprus (UNFICYP) role. The role involved the provision of an aerial resupply service and troop rotation to and from isolated observation posts.

With the increased need for helicopter support in West Germany, 72 Squadron was nominated as a stand-in unit for 18 Squadron and, on 11 December 1966, three Wessex of 72 Squadron were airfreighted in Shorts Belfast transport aircraft to Nicosia, to take over the tasking from 18 Squadron.

No. 230 Squadron returned on 18 April 1967 to relieve the Wessex, but their Whirlwind HAR Mk.10 aircraft quickly ran out of hours, requiring 72 Squadron to make an unscheduled return and take on the task again. Eventually, on

20 March 1968, 230 Squadron were back once more with reconditioned Whirlwind HAR Mk.10s and the Wessex were flown home overland – a distance of 2,200miles, taking some 21 hours to cover.

No. 72 Squadron returned again in February 1969, now with three aircraft augmented by UN markings. This would turn out to be the squadron's last deployment to Cyprus, with the Whirlwinds once again assuming the role and the Wessex returning to Odiham on 9 March 1970.

The closure of Nicosia and the relocation of all of its units to RAF Akrotiri had been announced in the 1966 Defence Review. On 17 February 1972, the Whirlwinds of 1563 Flight were rebadged under the re-formed 84 Squadron at Akrotiri with 'B' Flight being detached to Nicosia where they relieved the Wessex of the earlier 18 and 72 Squadron detachments.

28 (Army Co-operation) Squadron

In January 1972, 28 Squadron began receiving Wessex HC Mk.2s to operate initially alongside their Whirlwind HAR Mk.10 aircraft. With the last of the eight aircraft being delivered in August, the Whirlwinds were all returned to the UK, whereupon the Wessex became fully operational.

As with their predecessors, the Wessex were put to use in various roles in support of the local Hong Kong authorities and the RAF Regiment, primarily to police the 22-mile border of the New Territories. Each year, thousands of refugees from war-torn Vietnam and illegal immigrants from the neighbouring People's Republic of China attempted to get across the border to Hong Kong. This problem became worse with the warmer weather which only served to encourage those trying to get over.

LEFT Illegal Chinese immigrants being herded by soldiers from 1st Battalion the Royal Green Jackets aboard a 28 (AC) Squadron Wessex HC.2 on the border with Hong Kong in July 1979. *(Jonathan Falconer collection)*

ABOVE LEFT Wessex HC Mk.2s XT667 ('F') and XT678 ('H') in the 28 (AC) Squadron hangar at RAF Sek Kong, 10 June 1989. *(Tony Jupp)*

ABOVE Wessex HC Mk.2 XR522 ('A') of 28 (AC) Squadron taxies in to dispersal. A Nite Sun infrared light, used for searching for illegal immigrants at night, can be seen fitted to the starboard undercarriage. *(Pete Wendes)*

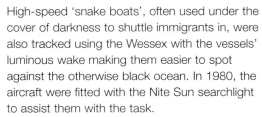

LEFT Wessex HC Mk.2 XT605 ('E') of 28 (AC) Squadron releases a cascade of water from the Sims Rainmaker firefighting bucket suspended from the aircraft's SACRU. *(Pete Wendes)*

High-speed 'snake boats', often used under the cover of darkness to shuttle immigrants in, were also tracked using the Wessex with the vessels' luminous wake making them easier to spot against the otherwise black ocean. In 1980, the aircraft were fitted with the Nite Sun searchlight to assist them with the task.

British Army units stationed along the border and on the outlying islands also benefited from a daily 'bus-run' transportation service, as well as the provision of casualty evacuation. Many soldiers were airlifted out for urgent medical attention after being bitten by snakes. Civilians were also flown out by the Wessex to nearby hospitals in emergencies.

As well as their military tasks, 'Hearts and Minds' tasks featured large in the squadron's repertoire. The lifting capabilities of the Wessex were put to use in providing assistance

with local civil engineering projects, carrying construction equipment and materials in to hard-to-reach areas of the colony to help with the building of schools and roads and generally improving the local infrastructure.

Firefighting also became an important role. The aircraft were fitted with the Sims Rainmaker firefighting bucket which had been used operationally for the first time in 1977. On 19 November 1979, XR508 and XR515 dropped a total of 72,000 gallons of water in 9 hours on the largest forest fire to have been tackled by helicopters to that date before it was brought under control.

Major servicing and modification work for the 28 Squadron aircraft was undertaken by the Hong Kong Aircraft Engineering Company (HAECO) at Kai Tak. The civilian company provided Wessex maintenance for both RAF and Royal Navy Wessex throughout the period of operation in the Far East alongside other military aircraft types and civil airliners.

On 17 May 1978, the squadron left Kai Tak ahead of the closure of the RAF base there, and moved to Sek Kong. The move put the squadron nearer to the border and provided it with more modern facilities. It returned, briefly, to Kai Tak in November 1996, where it finally disbanded on 3 June the following year, just ahead of the formal handover of the colony by Britain to the People's Republic of China.

With the Wessex being retired in the UK at the same time, there was no requirement to repatriate them and the surviving aircraft were instead all sold to Uruguay for operation with that country's Navy.

LEFT Wessex HC Mk.2 XR508 ('D') of 28 (AC) Squadron over the Hong Kong/ Chinese border. The stripe markings were added to increase the aircraft's in-theatre conspicuity. *(Pete Wendes)*

ABOVE 60 Squadron Wessex HC Mk.2 XV723 ('Q'). *(Author)*

LEFT The Markhor goat's head and lightning flash motif applied to the tail pylon of the 60 Squadron Wessex HC Mk.2s. *(Author)*

BELOW Flown into retirement: 60 Squadron Wessex HC Mk.2 XR502 ('Z') on arrival at NARO Fleetlands for final storage pending disposal, 13 January 1997. *(Author)*

60 Squadron

In March 1992, former 72 Squadron aircraft began to arrive at RAF Benson in advance of the formation of a new Wessex squadron. Most of the personnel working towards setting up the new, as-yet unnumbered unit assumed that it would be a re-formed 26 Squadron. It therefore came as something of a surprise when in May of that year it was announced that it would in fact be 60 Squadron.

With the unit's Markhor goat's head with lightning flashes adorning the tail pylon, the Wessex were used in the Support Helicopter role as well as providing an Operational Conversion Unit service to the other remaining operators.

As with the other remaining aircraft, 60 Squadron's Wessex were flown into retirement at Fleetlands in 1997 when the squadron disbanded.

72 Squadron

On 5 August 1964, 72 Squadron relinquished its previous aircraft, the Bristol Belvedere, and re-equipped with Wessex HC Mk.2s at RAF Odiham. Neighbouring 18 Squadron transferred its Wessex Conversion Flight element during November prior to leaving for Germany, whereupon 72 Squadron became the sole Short-Range Transport (SRT) helicopter squadron in the UK.

The Wessex were subsequently much in demand, providing assistance to UK national emergency and police services. In November

1966, the squadron was called upon to assist in the rescue operation following the Aberfan disaster in Wales, with one aircraft being sent to help lift heavy drilling equipment to the site.

On 22 March 1967, two Wessex were flown to RAF St Mawgan to take part in Operation Mop-Up – the effort to clean Cornish beaches of crude oil after the tanker *Torrey Canyon* had run aground four days earlier on the rocks of Seven Stone Reef. The Wessex joined the HU Mk.5s of 848 NAS and Station Flight Whirlwinds

ABOVE Wessex HC Mk.2 XR525 ('G') of 72 Squadron with original air intake door, call-sign on the nose and Transport Command titles.
(Author's collection)

LEFT Wessex HC Mk.2 XT671 ('W') of 72 Squadron at RAF Odiham, now fitted with the particle separator nose air intake, 1967.
(Graham Perry)

from RNAS Culdrose in conducting aerial reconnaissance, delivering films of the oil slick to Plymouth for analysis and load-lifting barrels containing oil-dispersing detergent to troops on the beaches and cliffs.

On 30 March, VIPs were flown out to witness the Fleet Air Arm Buccaneers and Hunters from Brawdy attacking the wreck of the ship with bombs and rocket projectiles in a bid to set fire to the oil slick and prevent it from spreading further. The operation continued well into April and, by the time it ended after 35 days, a total of some 3,351,810 tons of payload had been carried on 3,567 sorties over 297 flying hours.

Northern Ireland

In August 1969, following the deployment of the British Army on the streets of Northern Ireland in response to rioting throughout the province, 72 Squadron began its first deployment to RAF Aldergrove. Here, the aircraft were used to assist the military and civil authorities with conducting border patrols, providing an airborne delivery service and for troop training. For the Army, this was the beginning of Operation Banner; for the RAF, this was initially known as Operation Marginal.

No. 72 Squadron were briefly relieved by 18 Squadron between March and August 1970 in order to undertake an exercise in the Far East but, on their return, four aircraft were once again dispatched to Northern Ireland.

Operation Marginal was renamed as Operation Four Square in July 1971 and 72 Squadron were christened the 'Northern Ireland Detachment' in October that year. The flying rate had increased noticeably since the last deployment: in

December 1971 some 64,844lb of freight, 4,261 troops, 53 casualty evacuations and 19 VIPs were carried with flying hours totalling over 400.

Anywhere between four and eight aircraft would be deployed depending on the intensity of operations. In April 1972, a month which saw the planting of 24 bombs by the Provisional IRA in cities across Northern Ireland, this figure briefly went up to 12, resulting in 654 hours of flying being conducted – well over the allocated figure.

From December 1972, the arrival of Puma HC Mk.1s to replace some of 72 Squadron's aircraft saw the mixed-type deployment becoming collectively known as the 'RAF Helicopter Detachment Northern Ireland'.

During August 1977, a visit to Northern Ireland by Her Majesty the Queen led prison staff at The Maze prison to fear that inmates might set fire to their accommodation to achieve publicity. To combat this possibility, a Sims Rainmaker bucket was flown in specially from 18 Squadron at Gütersloh and a Wessex placed on firefighting standby at Long Kesh. The fears proved to be unfounded, however, and the equipment was later returned.

In late 1977, the Fleet Air Arm began sharing responsibility for the provision of helicopter support in Northern Ireland – now known as 'Support Helicopter Force Detachment Northern Ireland' (SHFDNI). No. 845 NAS flew four Wessex HU Mk.5s from RNAS Yeovilton to RAF Aldergrove on 10 October and 72 Squadron reduced to the same number. The Pumas would lose their Support Helicopter role in 1979, leaving just the combined Wessex squadrons to shoulder the responsibility.

Warrenpoint was to be the scene of a bombing during August 1979 in which one of 72 Squadron's Wessex, XR509, was damaged. Landing to pick up troops just 100yd from a second explosion, the aircraft's port windows were sucked out by the blast and the rotors hit by falling stones and masonry. Despite the proximity of the explosion, the aircraft managed to take off and landed safely at Bessbrook Mill shortly afterwards.

In April 1981, 72 Squadron moved from RAF Odiham to RAF Benson, Oxfordshire. However, the following November the arrival of the new twin-rotor Boeing Chinook HC Mk.1s triggered a chain reaction of aircraft reshuffling throughout the RAF. No. 18 Squadron swapped its Wessex HC Mk.2s for Chinooks, which in turn freed up sufficient numbers of the type to replace the venerable single-engined Whirlwind HAR Mk.10s in the SAR role.

This release of additional Wessex also saw the whole of 72 Squadron move to RAF Aldergrove to take over the Support Helicopter role with aircrew conducting two-year tours in what had recently been retitled 'Support Helicopter Force Northern Ireland' (SHFNI).

On 1 May 1982, the Wessex Training Flight (WTF) was disbanded at RAF Benson and all training was subsumed within the 72 Squadron frontline tasking. This coincided with 845 NAS being dispatched back to Yeovilton in preparation for sailing south as part of the Task Force to retake the Falkland Islands, leaving 72 Squadron to undertake all of the Northern Ireland tasking. A decision to send their own Wessex to the South Atlantic was reversed, but only after the aircraft had already flown to Benson.

No. 72 Squadron would remain in Northern Ireland throughout the next 15 years in support of the British Army and, in 1997, it became the last Wessex operator in the UK when 60 Squadron and the SAR aircraft were retired.

At 12.10pm on 25 March 2002, the last remaining ten aircraft finally departed Aldergrove bound for Odiham, leaving just one unserviceable aircraft – XR529 ('E') – behind to become a gate guardian at the base. Two days later the aircraft conducted a formation flypast along the Thames in London to Benson before setting course for their final destination, RAF Shawbury.

84 Squadron

At the end of February 1982, 84 Squadron in Cyprus finally retired the last of the RAF's Whirlwind HAR Mk.10s and re-equipped with Wessex HC Mk.2s to continue with providing both SAR and support to the UNFICYP.

The UNFICYP role involved helping to police the UN 'buffer' zone which stretched over 217km across the island, carrying out medical evacuations, conducting resupply missions for UN observation posts in the mountainous Sector 1 area, VIP flights, troop training for soldiers of the various troop contingents and providing a heavy-lift capability, lifting observation towers and water towers into position in parts of the country otherwise inaccessible by anything other than air. The responsibility eventually passed to the Alouette helicopters operated by the Army Air Corps (AAC) in October 1986.

BELOW First production Wessex HC Mk.2 XR588 still going strong with 84 Squadron at RAF Akrotiri just before the type's retirement from service in 2004. *(Author's collection)*

In parallel with this, the Wessex provided a SAR commitment primarily to the British Forces stationed on the island, but sometimes ventured further afield. Training was often conducted in Jordan and the aircraft were also on hand to help with evacuation of British nationals from war-torn Beirut.

Having initially worn their original UK SAR yellow paint scheme with roundels superimposed over a vertical band of UN pale blue on the tailcone to signify their primary role and to make them more conspicuous, the Wessex wore the squadron's adopted Arabian Scorpion motif, recognising their previous existence in the Middle East. Each aircraft also carried a suit of cards marking on the tail – Club, Diamond, Heart, Joker and Spade – which made them more identifiable from a distance, and by 1984 they had their yellow scheme replaced by a camouflage finish.

Following the withdrawal of both the RN's presence in Northern Ireland and a reduction of their Wessex commitments to SAR work, a number of HU Mk.5 aircraft became available. Beginning in late 1982, six aircraft were eventually converted at Royal Naval Aircraft Yard (RNAY) Fleetlands to HU Mk.5C standard.

The Mk.5Cs were deployed to Akrotiri from late 1982, allowing the standard HC Mk.2s to be returned to the UK. The aircraft differed from their predecessors in having the larger cabin windows and the Automatic Flight Control System (AFCS) 'coffin' in the forward port side of the cabin which doubled as a three-man seat. However, the years of being operated in predominantly salt-laden environments had taken their toll on the Mk.5Cs and their condition rapidly deteriorated, necessitating their own replacement by a fresh batch of HC Mk.2s by late 1995.

In the aftermath of the First Gulf War in 1991, colour scheme trials were conducted at

Brize Norton with aircraft appearing in a range of uniform colours including overall black and overall grey. While the Wessex of 72 Squadron received a two-tone green camouflage, the 84 Squadron aircraft were refinished in overall medium sea grey, still with their blue identification bands, squadron motifs and Union flag on the nose intake.

With the retirement of the type in both the UK and Hong Kong in 1997, 84 Squadron became the last operator of the Wessex. The aircraft soldiered on until 31 January 2003 when they were finally withdrawn from use, whereupon they were replaced by Bell Griffin helicopters provided under a Civil-Owned Military-Registered (COMR) contract.

The last four remaining aircraft, which included the very first RAF Wessex, XR588, were loaded aboard an An-124 transport aircraft at Akrotiri and flown to Brize Norton on 5 February. The aptly named 'Scorpion Formation' made the last British military flight of the Wessex on 20 February when they were flown from Brize to RAF Shawbury for storage pending disposal.

78 Squadron

In May 1965, the Wessex made a return to Aden, this time with the RAF. Nine HC Mk.2s of 72 Squadron broke away from its parent and

were shipped in Royal Fleet Auxiliary (RFA) *Sir Lancelot*, being transferred at RAF Khormaksar to re-equip the resident 78 Squadron.

The Wessex were engaged in night internal security operations in the highly dangerous Crater area, using a cordon and search tactic to drop off troops to surround an area suspected of containing dissident insurgents. The area would be systematically searched while armed AAC Scout helicopters prevented anyone from escaping.

Modified with searchlights and machine guns in both the starboard cabin door and through the port rear window aperture, the Wessex provided support to the Argyll and Sutherland Highlander British and South Arabian troops on the ground in policing the 'Scrubber Line' – the perimeter fence along the boundary of the Aden State. Ad hoc patrols were also carried out, looking for anything suspicious. Although the pilot's seat had an armour plate fitted beneath it, the second pilot (usually the new boys learning the ropes) had no such luxury. As one former squadron pilot later observed, 'sitting on one's flak-jacket was probably more a morale-booster than an effective defence'.

Operating conditions were no better for the HC Mk.2 than for the Royal Navy's HAS Mk.1s before them. But it wasn't just the aircraft that suffered. The heat in the cockpit and cabin of a

BELOW Against the backdrop of the mountains of the Radfan area of Aden, Wessex HC Mk.2 XS674 ('H') of 78 Squadron stops off for fuel supplied in drums, 1967.
(Peter Rawlings)

Wessex that had been standing in the sun for a couple of hours took its toll on aircrew, although once airborne the side windows and cabin door could at least be slid open to reduce the temperature. Each aircraft was dispatched with a coolbox containing drinks and the makings of sandwiches, but in the heat these quickly lost their effectiveness. Most aircrew would later recall runny butter being the order of the day. The engineers fared worse, having to work in and around heat-soaked airframes in the baking sun without the benefit of a cooling breeze.

One aircraft would remain overnight at Habilayn – as Thumier had by now been renamed – where the sound of gunfire was not unusual. The runway, which was of oiled sand, was often mined by the dissidents, and at one point a Beverley was damaged beyond repair having run over one of the mines. The Wessex operated from pierced steel planking (PSP) dispersals, so were not affected in the same way.

In 1967, with the situation in Aden having begun to rapidly deteriorate with the number of terrorist attacks trebling, the decision was taken to withdraw British forces from the country. Habilayn was duly handed over to the South Arabian Army on 26 June and, on 17 October, eight of the 78 Squadron Wessex left Aden aboard HMS *Fearless* bound for their new home at RAF Sharjah in the Trucial States where they arrived six days later. They were followed by the remaining six aircraft, this time in HMS *Intrepid*, leaving under cover of darkness on 25 November – Independence Day – to arrive on 4 December.

Just a year after their arrival at Sharjah, a much-needed programme of airfreighting the 78 Squadron Wessex back to the UK for complete overhaul at RNAY Fleetlands was begun to bring the aircraft back to a suitable condition.

BELOW Wessex HC Mk.2 XR500 ('A') of 78 Squadron conducting a rotors-running crew changeover aboard HMS *Intrepid* during the final withdrawal of British troops from Aden, 25 November 1967. *(Peter Rawlings)*

103 Squadron

In August 1972, 103 Squadron at the Singapore Armed Forces Base at Tengah began receiving the first of its new Wessex HC Mk.2s to replace its Whirlwind HAR Mk.10s. Crews arrived from the UK where they had undergone a conversion course with 240 Operational Conversion Unit (OCU) at Odiham. The last Whirlwind flypast took place on 31 October and the following day the unit became an entirely Wessex-equipped unit, finally being declared operational on 1 January 1973.

The squadron's role was to provide helicopter assistance to the joint Australian, New Zealand and British – ANZUK – Forces stationed in Singapore. Serviceability issues dogged the aircraft and it was not until August 1973 that a formation of all eight aircraft could be achieved.

No. 103 Squadron's existence was, however, to be short-lived. In the Defence Review of December 1974, the unit was initially earmarked to return to the UK along with most of the forces based in Singapore. When the decision was finalised three months later, however, that transfer order had changed to one of disbandment.

In the final few months, tasking was transferred from ANZUK HQ to direct control from the UK, supporting the School of Infantry Jungle Warfare, Royal Artillery and Gordon Highlanders.

The Wessex began being airfreighted back to the UK in July 1975 and, on completion of the final sortie on 31 July, 103 Squadron sent a signal to 28 Squadron in Hong Kong: 'You are now the best helicopter squadron in the Far East. Goodbye.' No. 103 Squadron disbanded the following day.

Search and rescue

In late 1967, an outbreak of foot and mouth disease in the UK had led to 72 Squadron cancelling all of its tasking, whereupon the squadron converted to a SAR role.

The change was unexpectedly fortuitous. On 7 December, the crash of one of the Queen's Flight Whirlwinds had led to the entire fleet of helicopters being grounded pending urgent checks. No. 38 Group quickly designated 72 Squadron to stand in for the 22 Squadron Whirlwinds while they were inspected and

ABOVE Wessex HC Mk.2 XT680 ('E') of 103 Squadron exercising with 1st Light Battery (The Blazers) RA during tactical Exercise U-Beaut in West Malaysia, 1973. *(Jonathan Falconer collection)*

deployed one Wessex to each of the six SAR stations – Chivenor, Valley, Acklington, Leconfield, Leuchars and Coltishall – with two additional aircraft remaining on standby at Odiham. During the one-month grounding order, three of the squadron's Wessex were scrambled on SAR operations.

Little did anyone know, but this was to be a foretaste of what would become a long-standing role played by the Wessex and one with which it would eventually become synonymous.

SAR Flight RAF Muharraq

Despite the final withdrawal of British troops from Aden in November 1967, the 8 Squadron Hawker Hunters remained in RAF Muharraq, Bahrain, in order to protect Kuwait from its aggressive Iraqi neighbours.

To provide the necessary SAR coverage for the unit, 78 Squadron detached its embedded SAR-configured Wessex to Muharraq to set up a separate Flight under the RAF's Gulf Communications and SAR Squadron – Gulf COMSAR.

Resplendent in what would later become the standard SAR scheme of overall golden yellow, the aircraft were instantly recognisable from any other SAR unit by the addition beneath the 'RESCUE' title on the tail with the words 'Rescue from the sea' in Arabic script. Crews

the winchman, Sergeant John Glanvill, the Air
Force Medal (AFM).

The SAR Flight was eventually disbanded in
May 1971 and the aircraft returned to the UK.
On 1 December 1967, 78 Squadron was itself
disbanded.

United Kingdom SAR

Back in the UK, both 22 and 202 Squadrons
had received their Whirlwinds back following
checks. As with all RAF and RN SAR units,
these aircraft were stationed at various coastal
locations to provide coverage primarily to
military aircraft in distress.

Providing civilian SAR coverage for the
English Channel, Bristow Helicopters Ltd
had been operating single Gnome-powered
Whirlwind Series 3 aircraft under contract to
the Department of Trade at RAF Manston. The
base also provided a cross-Channel customs-
clearance staging post for helicopters transiting
between the UK and West Germany in support
of the BAOR and an increase in traffic had led
to concerns over the provision of a suitable
SAR coverage. It was deemed, with little real
evidence to the contrary, that only a military-run
unit could do so adequately.

And so, in September 1974, two standard
HC Mk.2 aircraft (XR501 and XT602) were sent
to RNAY Fleetlands, Gosport, where they were
given yellow SAR paint finishes in preparation
for service with 72 Squadron 'D' Flight at Manston.

were expected to be airborne in the sweltering
heat and humidity within two minutes of being
scrambled, the aircraft having already been pre-
checked.

During the night of 18 May 1969, one of the
aircraft from Muharraq attended a stricken tug
which had caught fire while towing two barges
20 miles east of the base. In a 25kt wind, in
seas with a 6–7ft swell and with the ship ablaze
and likely to explode at any moment, all nine
of the tug's crew were winched to safety and
returned to land within one hour of take-off. For
their part in the operation, pilot Flying Officer
Maurice Bennée and navigator Flight Lieutenant
Kenneth Lloyd were both awarded the Queen's
Commendation for Valuable Service (QCVS) and

22 Squadron

In 1976, the RAF SAR Force underwent a complete reorganisation, heralding the start of the final phased replacement programme of the existing Whirlwind HAR Mk.10 aircraft with the Wessex. The Whirlwind had been a much-loved stalwart in the role, but its single Gnome engine left it vulnerable during over-water operations and it lacked the range required for some of the larger areas involved, notably the English Channel and the North Sea.

Beginning in May, the Whirlwind HAR Mk.10s of 22 Squadron were transferred entirely to 202 Squadron while 22 Squadron was re-equipped with the Wessex which, due to its dedicated role, became designated the Helicopter Air Rescue (HAR) Mk.2. As with 202 Squadron, 22 Squadron was divided into several letter-prefixed Flights to signify their locations: 22 Squadron 'A' Flight at RAF Chivenor and 'C' Flight at RAF Valley replaced their Whirlwinds with Wessex; 202 Squadron 'C' Flight at RAF Leuchars became 22 Squadron 'B' Flight; Leconfield became home to 'D' Flight, and 72 Squadron 'D' Flight at RAF Manston became 22 Squadron 'E' Flight.

Three months later, in September 1976, the RAF's Search and Rescue Wing at RAF Finningley was formed, taking overall control of the two helicopter SAR squadrons. It would not be until November 1981, however, that the Whirlwind was finally withdrawn from RAF use.

During the 1980s, the much more advanced Sea King HAR Mk.3 was introduced into service in the SAR role and it began to replace the Wessex in the longer-range operations.

In December 1988, two Wessex from 22 Squadron at RAF Valley were swiftly dispatched north of the border to Lockerbie to assist in the aftermath of the crash of PanAm Boeing 747 Flight 103.

The Wessex hit the headlines on 12 August 1993, when XR524 of 22 Squadron crashed into Llyn Padarn, a freshwater lake

ABOVE A welcome sight to anyone in distress: the winch operator of a Wessex HAR Mk.2 of 22 Squadron 'A' Flight Chivenor guides the winch wire during a rescue practice sortie, 11 May 1994.
(Peter J. Cooper)

BELOW Wessex HC Mk.2 XR507 of 22 Squadron wearing temporary SAR markings at RNAY Fleetlands, July 1981. *(Author's collection)*

RIGHT **Wessex HAR Mk.2 XV730 of SARTU RAF Valley conducting wet winch exercises off Anglesey.** *(Pete Wendes)*

in North Wales, during a training sortie from RAF Valley. The flotation equipment failed to activate as a result of a lack of salt in the water and three of the four young Air Training Corps cadets on board for an air experience flight failed to get out of the sinking aircraft and died, while the fourth cadet and the three crew members survived.

The inquiry into the crash later found that the tail rotor disconnect coupling had momentarily become disengaged during the simulated autopilot failure exercise. As the thrust of the tail rotor decreased, the coupling re-engaged, causing one of the driveshafts to fail under huge torsional shock loading, leading to loss of tail rotor drive and to the aircraft spinning out of control.

No. 22 Squadron finally relinquished its Wessex and replaced them with the Sea King HAR Mk.3 in 1995.

Search and Rescue Training Unit

Upon successfully passing out from the Central Flying School/2 Flying Training School rotary-wing training course at RAF Shawbury, aircrew rated above average were posted to the Search and Rescue Training Unit (SARTU) which was formed at RAF Valley in 1979 with six Wessex HC Mk.2s.

RIGHT **Wessex HC Mk.2 and HAR Mk.2, formerly of 60 and 72 Squadrons and SARTU in long-term storage at NARO Fleetlands, 1998.** *(Author)*

Here, they were given specialist training in operating the aircraft in the SAR role, honing their skills with cliff rescues and from RAF launches in the Irish Sea. Having passed the course, aircrew would be posted to the frontline with 22 Squadron, also at Valley.

In March 1997, SARTU relinquished the last of its yellow Wessex ahead of the unit becoming part of the civilian-run Defence Helicopter Flying School (DHFS) on 1 April. The remaining Wessex were all flown to the Naval Aircraft Repair Organisation (NARO, as it had now become) Fleetlands for storage before eventually being disposed of.

Training

The Short-Range Conversion Unit (SRCU) formed at Odiham on 5 August 1964 to train aircrew in Army Co-operation flying techniques. The SRCU included both fixed- and rotary-wing types, but at the end of June 1967 it disbanded with the Wessex HC Mk.2 element being re-formed as the Helicopter Operational Conversion Flight (HOCF).

On 1 May 1971, HOCF became the Air Training Squadron and then, on 30 December, it was rebadged as 240 OCU. On 3 November 1980, the aircraft came under the new WTF at RAF Benson.

The advent of the Falklands Conflict saw the disbandment of the WTF at the end of April 1982, whereupon the responsibility for the frontline training on type was transferred to 72 Squadron at Aldergrove.

LEFT Tail pylon markings of the Helicopter Operational Conversion Flight (HOCF) featuring the station badge of RAF Odiham. *(Author's collection)*

In 1992, the WOCF formed as part of 60 Squadron at Benson.

Central Flying School (CFS)/2 Flying Training School (FTS)

The RAF's CFS/2 FTS moved to Shawbury in 1976 and replaced its Whirlwind HAR Mk.10s with Wessex HC Mk.2s.

Distinctive with their red-painted nose intakes and red bands around the tailcone, the aircraft undertook advanced rotary-wing training for pilots and aircrewmen before they were selected either to go to SARTU for SAR training, or to one of the frontline units. As with most of the other Wessex units, 2 FTS disbanded on 1 April 1997.

BELOW Wessex HC Mk.2 XS679 ('WG') of CFS/2 FTS airborne from RAF Shawbury. *(Author's collection)*

Chapter Four

HCC Mk.4 – by royal appointment

The first helicopters to be used in connection with the British royal family were in fact the first helicopters to serve with the British armed forces: the Sikorsky R-4B Hoverfly. The first of these two-seat aircraft were delivered to The King's Flight at RAF Benson, Oxfordshire, in August 1947. Perhaps indicative of the way in which they were still viewed as something of a novelty, the helicopters were not used for the carriage of royal passengers but as aerial post delivery vans. Over the next two summers they saw service shuttling bags of mail that had been flown up from London to Dyce in one of the Flight's Vickers Viking aircraft to nearby Balmoral during the royal family's annual holiday.

OPPOSITE Finishing touches being applied to the immaculate paint on one of the Queen's Flight Wessex HCC Mk.4s (XV732) at RNAY Fleetlands, January 1993. (RNAY Fleetlands)

ABOVE **The original interior furnishings for the Queen's Flight Wessex HCC Mk.4.** (Leonardo Helicopters)

BELOW **With Westland's Chief Test Pilot, Ron Gellatly, looking on from far left, the last of the two Wessex HCC Mk.4s, XV733, is formally handed over to the Queen's Flight at Yeovil, 30 June 1969.** (Leonardo Helicopters)

Following the death of King George VI in 1952, The King's Flight was suitably retitled the Queen's Flight. Provided by the RAF, without charge to the Privy Purse, the aircraft of the Flight were intended for use specifically by Her Majesty the Queen. In reality, however, an early policy not to allow the sovereign to travel in rotary-wing aircraft meant that the Queen made very few flights in helicopters of any type, not least of which being those operating under her own name.

The first helicopters to equip the Flight for passenger use were specially built Alvis Leonides piston-engined Whirlwind HCC Mk.8s, based on the HAR Mk.5 and delivered in November 1960. Having taken an interest in helicopter flying several years earlier, and having been taught to fly the Whirlwind by the Fleet

Air Arm, HRH Prince Philip naturally went on to fly the Queen's Flight examples himself. These aircraft were later replaced by a pair of specially built Gnome-powered Whirlwind HCC Mk.12s resplendent in bright Signal Red with blue trim.

However, tragedy was to strike in 1967 when one of the Whirlwinds crashed after the main rotor head became detached during a transit flight. Although the crew were sadly killed, no VIPs were on board at the time.

With the Whirlwinds immediately grounded, a replacement was urgently needed. The Wessex was a natural successor to the Whirlwind. It benefited from twin-engine reliability, had better range and performance and it had a larger cabin. A single frontline Wessex was quickly reconfigured and pressed into temporary service. Although the Whirlwind grounding order was eventually lifted, the remaining HCC Mk.12 never operated with the Queen's Flight again and was soon disposed of.

Order placed

On 22 February 1968, an order for two specially equipped aircraft to Specification 267 D&P and designated as HCC Mk.4 was announced in the House of Commons. The timescale for production of the aircraft was incredibly tight. The formal contract was signed on 28 June and the first example, XV732, made its maiden flight in the hands of Test Pilot Roy Moxam at Yeovil on 17 March 1969, followed on 13 May by XV733, flown by his colleague Peter Wilson.

As per their predecessors, the aircraft were finished in high-gloss Signal Red with dark blue cheat line, Light Aircraft Grey undercarriage oleos, the royal cipher on the cabin door (later with Union flag on the tail pylon), and highly polished exhausts and chrome fittings. These were indeed elegant-looking machines befitting their role.

The HCC Mk.4's original VVIP interior, costing the – appropriately enough – princely sum of £7,000, featured seven forward-facing VIP seats, improved soundproofing and larger windows. However, just a year after entering service, proposals were put forward to alter the layout to make better use of the spacious cabin. Interior specialists Rumbolds, who were renowned for producing airline furnishings, proposed two aft-facing double 'Slimline' seats with hydraulic

reclining mechanisms and seatbelts and the replacement of the central seats with two foldable Pullman tables. At a time when a new two-bedroomed semi-detached house would cost in the region of £1,000, one horrified Treasury official noted his incredulity over the quoted £1,260 bill, asking, 'Are we buying the tables from Christies – are they specially [sic] valuable antique tables – Chippendales, perhaps?'

Unlike the standard military variants, the cockpit incorporated what could be likened to the Global Positioning System (GPS) of its day – a Decca Mk.19 rolling map display. After trials at Boscombe Down, both aircraft entered service with the Queen's Flight, operating under No. 38 Group, RAF Benson, on 27 June that year, on which date the first royal flight occurred when Their Royal Highnesses the Duke and Duchess of Kent were flown from Maidstone to Coppins in XV732. The first official outing for the aircraft, however, was during the investiture of HRH Prince Charles as Prince of Wales at Caernarfon Castle on 1 July 1969.

During the 1970s and 1980s, the Duke of Edinburgh, Prince of Wales and, latterly, the Duke of York – all qualified helicopter pilots in their own right – would often fly the aircraft themselves to and from engagements in order to maintain proficiency.

Although Her Majesty the Queen rarely flew in the aircraft, many senior royals did so on a regular basis, most notably Her Majesty the Queen Mother, who was a regular passenger. But more usually they were commandeered by the Prime Minister of the day, Foreign and Commonwealth Secretary, First Secretary of State, Home Secretary, Secretaries of State for Defence, Scotland and Wales, the Ministers of Defence and the Parliamentary Under-Secretaries of State for Defence, the Chiefs of Staff and the General Officer Commanding London District, all of whom were eligible to make use of the aircraft for official business.

Journeys were rarely of more than 200 miles, but occasionally included destinations as far afield as Germany. All other requests to use the aircraft had to be given approval by the sovereign herself.

On 31 March 1995, the Queen's Flight officially disbanded at RAF Benson and the aircraft transferred to RAF Northolt as part of 32 (The

ABOVE In March 1995, the Queen's Flight disbanded and the Wessex were transferred to 32 (The Royal) Squadron at RAF Northolt, whose badge was later added to the cabin door. *(Author)*

ABOVE Original royal cipher and title applied to the cabin door on XV733, now protected at the International Helicopter Museum by a Perspex panel. *(Author)*

Royal) Squadron 'A' Flight. The honour of carrying out the last royal flight went to XV732 on 25 March 1998. Both aircraft were subsequently flown to RAF Shawbury the following month for long-term storage pending disposal.

Thankfully, both examples of these fine machines were to find new homes: XV732 with the RAF Museum at Hendon and XV733 with the International Helicopter Museum at Weston-super-Mare, where they can be seen to this day.

BELOW HRH Princess Margaret alighting from one of the Queen's Flight Wessex. *(Author's collection)*

Chapter Five

Royal Navy HU Mk.5

Although the HAS Mk.1, in the utility role, had served the Commando units of the Fleet Air Arm well during the start of the Indonesian Confrontation, it was still an anti-submarine design, not specifically a troop carrier. As with operations over the sea, its single Gazelle engine rendered it extremely vulnerable when flying over the dense jungles of Borneo. But the advent of the RAF's twin Gnome-engined HC Mk.2 paved the way for a Royal Navy version with a greater safety margin and an improved load-lifting capacity. The result was the Wessex HU (Helicopter Utility) Mk.5.

OPPOSITE Using skills previously honed in the Far East, Wessex HU Mk.5 XT482 ('ZM/VL') of 707 NAS conducts confined area landings at RNAS Merryfield. *(RNAS Yeovilton)*

ABOVE Wessex HU Mk.5 XS479 ('A/A') of 848 NAS perched on a landing pad built from sandbags and logs while delivering supplies to Gurkha troops in Borneo, November 1965.
(Leonardo Helicopters)

The first production order for the HU Mk.5 was placed on 28 August 1962 consisting of 40 aircraft. A single HU Mk.5 prototype, XS241, was also built at Yeovil and made its first flight there on 31 May 1963 in the hands of Leo De Vigne ahead of the first production aircraft that November; 60 more examples were ordered between June 1964 and February 1965 with the final one, XT774, being delivered in 1967.

700V NAS

No. 700V NAS formed at RNAS Culdrose on 29 October 1963 as the Wessex HU Mk.5 IFTU. It disbanded on 7 May 1964 and promptly became the new 848 NAS.

848 NAS

The first squadron to equip with the Wessex HU Mk.5 was 848 NAS which was quickly

RIGHT No. 845 NAS Wessex HU Mk.5 XT460 ('T/A') during the rescue of British Nationals from Cyprus, July 1974.
(via Gary Savage)

dispatched to the Far East to relieve 845 NAS and their Wessex HAS Mk.1s operating in Borneo. No. 845 was eventually relieved itself by the re-equipped 848 NAS in 1966.

845 NAS

In October 1964, 845 NAS re-equipped with the Wessex HU Mk.5 and in 1966 sailed in HMS *Bulwark* for Borneo. The squadron finally left the Far East, again in HMS *Bulwark*, in 1968.

707 NAS

No. 707 NAS re-formed with Wessex HU Mk.5s at Culdrose in December 1964. Its role was that of providing Advanced and Operational Flying Training (AFT/OFT) to RN and Royal Marine aircrew, as well as undertaking operational development trials work and exercising with the Army.

In May 1972, the squadron moved to Yeovilton where, a decade later, it spawned 848 NAS for service in the Falklands Conflict. The Wessex began being replaced by the Sea King HC Mk.4 later the following year with the task of providing Commando instruction on the Wessex being passed to 771 NAS in September 1985.

846 NAS

Re-formed in 1968 as a Wessex HU Mk.5 unit, 846 NAS initially undertook camouflage trials in which a number of temporary schemes were tried out. Although 'Devon Red' proved to be surprisingly effective, Olive Drab was eventually chosen as the colour for all future Commando helicopters.

In May 1972, the squadron moved to

ABOVE Wessex HU Mk.5 XT454 ('L/B') of 845 NAS operating over Aden in 1966. *(Author's collection)*

LEFT Soon after re-forming with Wessex HU Mk.5s, 846 NAS undertook camouflage trials which included XS480 ('B/CU') seen here in a 'Devon Red' finish. *(Author's collection)*

GREEN PARROTS AND RED DRAGONS

In 1969, 781 NAS at RNAS Lee-on-Solent began replacing the last of its ageing piston-engined VIP-fit Whirlwind HAS Mk.22 helicopters with two Wessex HU Mk.5s. Inheriting from their predecessors the affectionate name of the 'Green Parrots' due to their smart Grass Green-painted fuselages, white upper surfaces and gold cheat line, these aircraft were employed on a variety of tasks often involving trips in and

out of Battersea Heliport in London, shuttling admirals and cabinet ministers to and from high-level meetings.

Their cabins had been fitted out at RNAY Fleetlands with pale green airline-type seating, tables, grey carpeting, red curtains and soundproofing as well as an additional window in the sliding door to allow more light in, and were ordinarily kept in 'Q' Hangar at Lee, separate from the squadron's Sea Devon and Sea Heron fixed-wing communications aircraft. Unlike these, the Wessex were maintained not by civilians under contract but by military personnel.

Although only two aircraft were normally on strength at any one time, between 1969 and March 1981 when the squadron was finally disbanded, a total of four of these Wessex had been converted and used in the role at various times. With the unit falling victim to defence cuts, the aircraft were subsumed within normal

LEFT The interior of one of the 781 NAS 'Green Parrot' Wessex HU Mk.5s. *(RNAY Fleetlands)*

RIGHT HRH Prince Charles in the cockpit of one of the specially allocated Wessex HU Mk.5s of 707 NAS Red Dragon Flight, whose badge he wears on his right shoulder. *(Author's collection)*

frontline units and stripped of their special interiors and eventually their colourful markings.

In July 1974, a three-month conversion course was devised by 707 NAS under the name of 'Red Dragon Flight' to provide training for HRH the Prince of Wales. Two Wessex HU Mk.5s were selected and marked with large areas of Day-Glo to increase their visibility and components were changed at half-lives instead of the normal periodicities. On completion of the training in December, Red Dragon Flight transferred to 845 NAS along with its newly qualified pilot.

BELOW Wessex HU Mk.5 XT773 ('B') of 707 NAS Red Dragon Flight undertaking wet winching practice. *(Author's collection)*

ABOVE Parachutists
jumping from Wessex
HU Mk.5 XT469 ('E/S')
of 847 NAS based at
RNAS Sembawang.
(Author's collection)

Yeovilton but disbanded in 1977 with the aircraft
being pooled with those of 845 NAS.

No. 846 NAS re-formed again in October
1978, seeing service in HMS *Hermes* and HMS
Bulwark, but Sea King HC.4s began to replace
it two months later and the Wessex were
eventually disposed of in October 1981.

847 NAS

No. 847 NAS formed at RNAS Sembawang,
Singapore, in March 1969 and was unusual
in never returning to the UK throughout its
commission. It saw use during the flood relief
operations in Pakistan in 1970 and later in
western Malaysia before being disbanded in May
1971 with the aircraft transferring to 848 NAS.

Exercise Clockwork

In 1969, the Commando helicopter squadrons
of the Fleet Air Arm made the first of what was
to become an annual trip across the North Sea
to the barren wastes of Norway and the Royal
Norwegian Air Force base at Bardufoss to
undertake Exercise Clockwork.

Situated 140 miles north of the Arctic Circle,
conditions here during winter are harsh with
deep snow and temperatures often plummeting
below –30°C. In these challenging conditions,
aircrew and maintainers were taught to live,
fly and fight with their aircraft providing aerial
transport and load-lifting for the Royal Marine

LEFT Ground troops preparing to 'hook on'
an underslung load to Wessex HU Mk.5 XT760
('VS/B') of 846 NAS. Note the recirculating
snow kicked up by the main rotor downwash.
(via David Baston)

troops who were tasked with protecting the northern flank of NATO.

Having just returned from the Far East, Norway was something of a shock to the system. With snow everywhere, navigating over featureless, white terrain was demanding. Landings and take-offs were no less of a challenge. The lighter and fluffier the snow, the more difficult it became, as former Wessex pilot John Beattie recalls:

Take-off was simple, but when coming into the hover the snow cloud kicked up blotted out all normal visual references and disorientation was not very far away. Landing whilst focussing on an object that stood out was the way to do it, be it a small tree, rock, or perhaps a couple of troops you were about to pick up. If there wasn't anything, we would make a low, slow pass and throw a Bergen out of the door as a visible 'feature' to land on from the next approach.

In the winter months, the sun remained below the horizon and everything was fairly gloomy, often with no visible horizon, again leading to ideal disorientation conditions against the generally white background and relying on instruments became more important.

ABOVE A Wessex HU Mk.5 of 848 NAS on loan to 846 NAS up to the axles in snow in Norway, retrieving troops during Arctic training. The aircraft is fitted with the 'upside down' cold-running nose air intake. *(Author's collection)*

BELOW A Wessex HU Mk.5 of 845 NAS bringing in supplies to Bessbrook Mill, Northern Ireland, 1980. *(Author's collection)*

ABOVE No. 845
NAS conducting
troop movements
from Crossmaglen,
Northern Ireland,
during 1980. The
dog beneath the
aircraft appears not
to be bothered by the
sight and sound
of a Wessex!
(Author's collection)

More demanding, perhaps, was the need to carry out maintenance on the helicopters in cold temperatures. At below −15°C, hands stick to metal and simple functions become difficult. Building a tent over the engine bays with a disused parachute and filling it with warm air from a heater would allow an engine change to be carried out, for instance. Rotor blades were seriously affected by icing in certain conditions, so they were liberally coated with what we delightfully termed 'Gorilla snot', an anti-icing agent in the form of a gel. The aircraft mechanical components could suffer dissimilar metal contraction below −26°C. If such temperatures were forecast, aircraft were run or heated throughout the night to keep gearboxes above the critical temperatures.

Engine intakes could accrete ice, which then tended to break off and get sucked in, trashing the rather delicate compressor blades. To get around this problem a heated door was designed, but with an intake 'upside down' to the normal. It worked well in terms of providing heated intake air but acted rather like a vacuum cleaner, sucking anything in that moved. It caused a lot of engine changes before it was put in a museum. We all carried a fully packed Bergen in the back of the aircraft, in case we went down in inhospitable terrain, giving the ability to survive for weeks if necessary. Thankfully, no one ever had to.

Falklands – 845, 847 and 848 NAS

On 1 April 1982, the Wessex was prepared to go off to war. No. 845 NAS, at that stage the only frontline Wessex unit, had its complement of 22 Wessex HU Mk.5 aircraft split between their Yeovilton base and Aldergrove where they were supporting the British Army along with their RAF counterparts. Plans were immediately put in place to return the aircraft to the mainland and begin embarkation in ships as part of the Task Force.

No. 845 NAS embarked 14 of its aircraft in RFA *Resource*, RFA *Fort Austin* and RFA *Tidespring*, as well as HMS *Intrepid*, split into five lettered Flights: A to E. A further six aircraft were airfreighted out to Ascension Island in civilian Belfast aircraft. Those aircraft and aircrew returning from Aldergrove to Yeovilton would be diverted to re-form as 847 NAS.

Meanwhile, the two aircraft of 'B' Flight had been embarked in the container ship SS *Atlantic Conveyor* for the journey south. On 25 May, the ship was hit by two air-launched Exocet missiles and began to burn fiercely. One of 'B' Flight's aircraft, XT468, had been airborne at the time undergoing a test flight and on returning managed to pick up survivors from the ship before landing aboard HMS *Hermes*. The other Wessex, XS512, had just completed a ground run on deck but the intense heat had prevented anyone from getting near to her and she, along with all of the 848 NAS 'D' Flight Wessex and all but one RAF Chinook – also airborne at the time – went down with the ship.

'C' Flight, embarked in RFA *Tidespring*, had meanwhile been making its way to South Georgia in company with HMS *Antrim* and a team of SAS soldiers with the aim of retaking the island from Argentinian forces. Having landed the troops on the top of Fortuna Glacier, guided through atrocious weather by *Antrim*'s radar-equipped Wessex HAS Mk.3 XP142 'Humphrey', the aircraft were forced to return the next day in even worse conditions to pick the men up again who were in real danger of succumbing to the weather. As the two aircraft started their descent, first XT473, then XT464 became enveloped in white-out conditions and crashed, luckily with no fatalities. With no

option but to cram the survivors into the cabin alongside the sonar equipment, 'Humphrey' would fly to the ship and back again to collect the remainder. The wreckage of the two 845 NAS aircraft were left where they fell and indeed remain there to this day.

An aircraft from 'E' Flight, operating temporarily from SS *Canberra*, would see action on 21 May following the bombing of HMS *Ardent* by Argentinian aircraft. In the aircraft was Surgeon Commander Rick Jolly who volunteered himself to be lowered into the freezing water twice without an immersion suit to grab two struggling survivors.

On 11 June, the crew of XT484 from 845 'A' Flight attempted to hit Port Stanley Town Hall under cover of darkness with AS.12 missiles having received intelligence that it was being used by the Argentinian high command. The missiles missed their target by feet and instead hit the neighbouring police station, prompting the Wessex to come under sustained enemy attack but it managed to make its getaway unscathed. Unbeknown to the crew, the building was actually being used as a headquarters for Argentinian intelligence, so the mission achieved some success.

847 NAS

On 7 May, 847 NAS was quickly re-formed from elements of 771 and 772 NAS. With some 24 aircraft mustered into two Flights – 'A' and 'B' – they embarked for the journey south just nine days later.

On 8 June, XT480 was involved in the rescue of survivors from RFA *Sir Galahad* at Port Pleasant. The ship, full of Welsh Guards, had been bombed while at anchor and was ablaze. In company with Sea Kings of 825 NAS, the Wessex made use of its rotor downwash by blowing dinghies away from the ship to safety.

In September, 847 NAS became the Falkland Islands detachment, finally returning home to the UK in December.

848 NAS

The second Wessex squadron to be re-formed for Operation Corporate was 848 NAS which came into being on 17 April as a frontline unit by effectively upgrading 707 NAS, the Wessex

training unit, and augmenting it with aircraft from 772 NAS.

As with the other squadrons, 848 NAS was split into lettered Flights – 'A' to 'D'. While 'A' Flight was involved in the successful recapture of Southern Thule on 20 June, 'D' Flight never made it to the Falklands. All six aircraft had been embarked in SS *Atlantic Conveyor* and, as with the aircraft from 845 'A' Flight, went to the bottom of the Atlantic with the ship after it was hit by Exocet missiles.

Nos. 845, 847 and 848 NAS flew a combined 4,757 hours over 1,841 sorties and conducted 2,698 deck landings during Operation Corporate, bettered only by the

ABOVE The one that nearly got away; XS512 ('WT') of 848 NAS 'D' Flight sits on the deck of SS *Atlantic Conveyor*, which was hit by an Argentinian Exocet missile shortly after the aircraft had returned from a test flight. Unfortunately, the aircraft went down with the ship on 30 May 1982.
(Author's collection)

RIGHT An impressive line-up of Wessex HU Mk.5s of 771 NAS taxying out at RNAS Culdrose in call-sign numerical order.
(RNAS Culdrose)

newer Sea King HAS Mk.5s of 820 and 826 NAS. The HAS Mk.3s of HMS *Antrim* and HMS *Glamorgan*, meanwhile, flew a combined total of 333 hours 25 minutes, 213 sorties and completed 522 deck landings. A detached Flight of 845 NAS Wessex was maintained at Ascension Island for a while afterwards, being used to ferry passengers and stores between ships supplying the Falkland Islands and the airliners connecting with the United Kingdom.

Search and rescue

No. 772 NAS at Portland re-equipped with the HU Mk.5 in 1976 and 771 NAS at Culdrose followed suit in 1979. The list of brave and heroic rescue operations undertaken by the crews of the SAR units over the next decade is long and impossible to detail here, but a few notable events are worthy of special mention.

Perhaps the best known of all SAR operations in which Royal Navy Wessex were involved occurred in August 1979 when four HU Mk.5s of 771 NAS (XT467, XT474, XT482 and XT761) were used in the rescue of yachtsmen during the Fastnet Race. Over 300 yachts got into severe difficulties in horrendous storm-force weather which led to the deaths of 18 individuals. One of the 771 NAS Wessex pilots, Lieutenant Jerry Grayson, was later awarded the Air Force Cross for his part in the rescue operation.

The date of 11 August 1985 proved to be a particularly busy day for 771 NAS at Culdrose. Early that morning a crew led by Lieutenant David Marr and Petty Officer Michael Palmer

were scrambled in Force 9 winds to assist the yacht *Mister Cube*, which had run into difficulties 55 miles off The Lizard. RN diver, Petty Officer Larry Slater, was winched down

No. 50453   3447

SECOND SUPPLEMENT TO

The London Gazette

of Monday, 10th March 1986

Published by Authority

Registered as a Newspaper

TUESDAY, 11TH MARCH 1986

MINISTRY OF DEFENCE

HONOURS AND AWARDS

NAVY DEPARTMENT

CENTRAL CHANCERY OF
THE ORDERS OF KNIGHTHOOD
St. James's Palace, London S.W.1
11th March 1986

The QUEEN has been graciously pleased to approve the award of the George Medal to:

Petty Officer Aircrewman Laurence SLATER, D114895W

Petty Officer Aircrewman Slater was the duty Diver of a Search and Rescue Wessex helicopter crew which was scrambled at 0730 on 11th August 1985 to assist the yacht *Mister Cube*, disabled in severe gale conditions approximately 55 miles south-east of Lizard Point.

Weather at the scene was sea state 7 with the wind gusting over 50 knots. The yacht was being pounded by 25 foot waves, its sails shredded, masts whipping violently through arcs of over 90° and the hull was lurching heavily in the severe swell.

With considerable difficulty, a light line was passed from the helicopter to the yacht. This was attached to Petty Officer Slater on the end of the helicopter's rescue winch. The helicopter was thus able to hover clear to one side of the yacht, while Slater was lowered on the winch and simultaneously pulled in on the yacht. Fighting his way past sails and whipping rigging he eventually reached the cockpit to find six children and three adults. He quickly reassured everyone and briefed them comprehensively on the rescue method.

Three older children were single lifted to safety. On two occasions, as Slater started double lifting the younger children, severe yacht movement caused the light line to part.

For the fifth time he was transferred to the deck, organising the single lift of two adults, but, as he returned for the final rescue the yacht was knocked onto its beam ends by a giant wave. Miraculously Slater and the last survivor managed to hang on long enough for the aircraft to position itself and lift them clear. Once away from the yacht, Slater calmly cut the light line and winched the survivor into the aircraft. The aircraft returned to R.N.A.S. Culdrose at 0925.

Later that same day, at 1510, Slater was again launched as part of a Search and Rescue crew sent to the assistance of a Fastnet Race casualty, the yacht *Drum England*, capsized off Porthscatho. On arrival 18 survivors were found crouching precariously on the upturned hull. They indicated that a further six persons were either missing or trapped inside.

Despite a sea state 5 and wind gusting 36 knots, the immediate danger necessitated Slater jumping from the aircraft and free swimming to the vessel.

Totally fearless, and disregarding his own safety, Slater dived beneath the jerking hull. Fighting his way past alarming snarls of torn sail and a tangled array of rigging, he came upon a rope locker and a white hatch. On forcing the hatch open he swam into an accommodation space, and was pulled into an air pocket by the missing survivors.

Despite the eerie situation, his exceptional courage, professionalism and outstanding presence enabled him swiftly to reassure and efficiently brief an escape plan. Remarkably, Slater safely extricated all six, pulling them out past a maze of rigging before returning each to the surface. Slater then remained on board supervising the winch evacuation of 20 survivors.

Throughout both of these exceptionally hazardous rescue operations Slater totally disregarded his own safety. The rescue of 29 people under the most arduous conditions in two very demanding situations on the same day was accomplished due to the great fearlessness, superb stamina and unflinching courage of Petty Officer Aircrewman Slater in the face of enormous danger.

from the cabin and managed to recover all three adults and nine children to the Wessex.

Just six hours later a further call came in for the capsized yacht *Drum England*, owned by Simon Le Bon of the pop group Duran Duran – yet another casualty of the Fastnet Race. Yet again, Petty Officer Slater and Petty Officer Palmer, this time with Lieutenant Coles as pilot, raced to the scene to find 18 people clinging to the upturned hull with a further six trapped inside. Having recovered those from the outside of the yacht, Slater then dived under the surface and found his way inside the hull where he found six men, including Le Bon, in an air pocket. Dragging each of them out, all six were eventually winched to safety. For his heroic rescue work, Slater was later awarded the George Medal. Marr and Palmer were both awarded Queen's Commendations for Valuable Service in the Air.

Retirement

In March 1988, the Royal Navy finally retired the last of its Wessex HU Mk.5s. While some were disposed of to museums, most of the aircraft were sent to the Air Engineering School (AES) at RNAS Lee-on-Solent where they joined some of their HAS Mk.1 and HAS Mk.3 siblings to be used as ground instructional airframes for teaching new naval aeronautical engineers.

This new life saw many of the aircraft being kept in fully functional condition in order for the various systems to be explained and practical skills to be honed. Others were less fortunate, being allocated for battle damage repair

LEFT Many others were used by the Air Engineering School (later DCAE) at both RNAS Lee-on-Solent and HMS *Sultan* for systems training and also for battle damage repair, resulting in large areas of new and repaired skins. *(Author)*

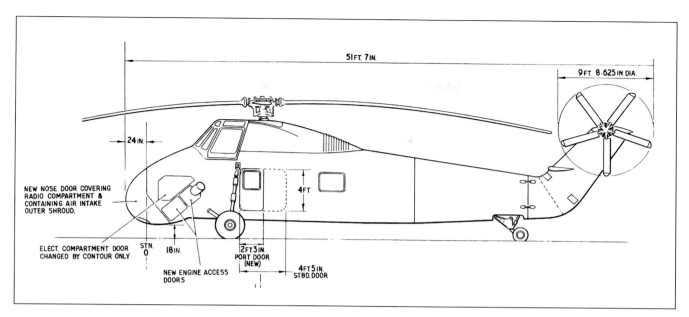

Schematic dimensions shown on diagram:
51FT. 7IN.
9FT. 8·625 IN. DIA.
24 IN.
4FT
NEW NOSE DOOR COVERING RADIO COMPARTMENT & CONTAINING AIR INTAKE OUTER SHROUD.
ELECT. COMPARTMENT DOOR CHANGED BY CONTOUR ONLY
STN. 0
18 IN.
NEW ENGINE ACCESS DOORS
2FT 3 IN. PORT DOOR (NEW)
4FT 5 IN. STBD. DOOR

training. Here, random holes were punched into the sides of the airframe that the students then had to repair using only basic tooling and materials – an essential skill needed when operating aircraft away from base.

Not long after the AES moved to nearby HMS *Sultan*, the Wessex began to be replaced by redundant Sea King airframes in the same role. Many of the aircraft were, by now, in a poor state after years of use. Several can now be found in paintball parks and even submerged in lakes as artificial diving reefs, or converted to 'glamping chalets'.

Wessex Mk.6

In March 1965, proposals were put forward by Westlands to satisfy Naval and Air Staff Target (NAST) 365 requirement for prolonging the life of existing Wessex HC Mk.2s and HU Mk.5s, or to replace them both with a new variant. The plans were dubbed 'Wessex Mk.6'.

The first of two designs involved the rebuild of existing HC Mk.2 and HU Mk.5 aircraft with an all-up weight (AUW) of 14,000lb, increased chord main rotor blades, and an additional 2ft 3in-wide door on the port side of the cabin. A five-bladed tail rotor with larger diameter would increase the aircraft length to 51ft 7in and height to 14ft 8.25in.

The second was more radical, featuring a larger cabin with redesigned tailcone and

pylon, port cabin door, redesigned four-bladed tail rotor and Sikorsky S-61-type main undercarriage including fuel cells carried in each sponson.

As part of the feasibility study, XS241 had been flown to the Aircraft and Armament Experimental Establishment (A&AEE) at Boscombe Down in July 1965 and fitted with a Sikorsky S-61 tail rotor hub featuring five standard Wessex tail rotor blades, increasing the tail rotor diameter by 2.5in, in a bid to determine whether it provided any improvement in yaw control at high-pitch angles. But ultimately the plans were abandoned in favour of procuring the SH-3D design the following year and anglicising it, ultimately emerging as the Westland Sea King.

ABOVE Schematic of the proposed Wessex Mk.6, showing the changes including the five-bladed tail rotor which was later test-flown on XS241. *(Leonardo Helicopters)*

BELOW Wessex HU Mk.5 prototype XS241 flying with the five-bladed tail rotor intended for the Wessex Mk.6. *(Leonardo Helicopters)*

Chapter Six

Mk.60 – civil Wessex

In a confidential internal report dated 23 February 1962, the Technical Director of Research at Westland proposed that the use of a small transport helicopter to carry passengers, freight, mail and emergency services on feeder line routes such as the islands off the Scottish coast and in underdeveloped countries might be met by a civil version of the Gnome-powered Wessex. Although noting that the use of gas turbine engines in civil helicopters was still in its early stages and, as such, civil registration was proving to be difficult, it was suggested that market research should be conducted and a brochure produced. The result would ultimately be the Wessex Mk.60.

OPPOSITE Wessex Mk.60 G-ATBY taking off from British Petroleum's Sea Gem North Sea oil rig. *(Leonardo Helicopters)*

ABOVE Wessex Mk.60
G-ASWI, operating
under Bristow
contract to Amoco,
approaching the oil
drilling platform 'Mr
Louie' in
the North Sea.
(Leonardo Helicopters)

Plans to produce a civilian version of the
Wessex had actually been tabled as far back
as 1959 when a 12- and 14-seat variant was
proposed by Westland. Based on what would
become the coupled Gnome-powered Wessex
HC Mk.2, the aircraft would have featured
a cabin heater, an additional door aft on the
port side of the fuselage to access a baggage
or mail compartment and two large 16cu ft
baggage canisters mounted one on either side
on struts above the mainwheels with hinged
access doors.

However, there remained one problem: the
acceptance of gas turbine-powered helicopters
by the Air Registration Board (ARB) – the
predecessor of the Civil Aviation Authority
(CAA). Up to this point, civilians had operated
only piston-engined helicopters, with gas
turbines being very much a military preserve.
Proving that non-military operators had the
necessary skills and infrastructure to maintain

these still relative new forms of helicopter
propulsion would be something of a struggle.

Bristow Helicopters Ltd

The key to the development and success
of civil, gas turbine-engined helicopters
lay in the discovery and subsequent wholesale
exploration of oil and gas reserves in the North
Sea beginning in the early 1960s. And it was
one company in particular that would become
synonymous with providing helicopters for this
very purpose: Bristow.

Alan Bristow was a larger-than-life former
Fleet Air Arm pilot who had been one of the first
to undertake the earliest helicopter trials in the
UK with Sikorsky Hoverflies in the late 1940s.
After leaving the Royal Navy, he briefly joined
Westland Aircraft Ltd as a test pilot before flying
helicopters in war-torn Indochina. Returning to
the UK, he formed Air Whaling Ltd, providing

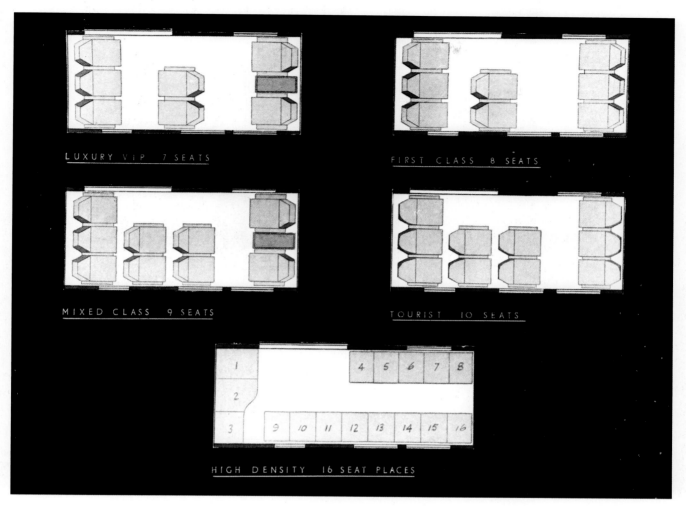

LUXURY VIP 7 SEATS

FIRST CLASS 8 SEATS

MIXED CLASS 9 SEATS

TOURIST 10 SEATS

HIGH DENSITY 16 SEAT PLACES

ABOVE The seating configuration options for the Wessex Mk.60. (Leonardo Helicopters)

diminutive Hiller helicopters to ships operated by whaling companies to assist in spotting their quarry in the Antarctic during the early 1950s. In 1955, the company had been reborn to bear his name: Bristow Helicopters Ltd (BHL).

Among many other achievements, BHL were to pioneer the use of helicopters in the civil market and gain commercial-type certificates for aircraft which had, until that point, only been deemed capable of being operated by military users. It had rapidly become the world's largest civil operator of helicopters, taking on support contracts for oil rigs in all manner of inhospitable and far-flung places including the Middle East, Brazil, Australia, Africa, Trinidad and Peru.

For many years, rumours had persisted about the potential for finding large oil deposits deep under the North Sea which, if exploited, could bring huge financial as well as domestic benefits to the UK, which was still reliant upon expensive foreign imports. But unlike most

of the other operations around the world, the potential drilling positions were a long way offshore. The weather in the North Sea was notoriously unpredictable and dangerous, and helicopters such as the Whirlwind simply did not have the load-carrying capability, the range or the endurance to conduct the transit flights with any meaningful passenger or cargo loads. They were also single-engined. If one were to have engine failure while carrying a maximum number of passengers in atrocious weather, the chances of being rescued were slim. What was needed was an aircraft with twin engines and a greater all-round performance.

Wessex Mk.60

In early 1965, BHL announced the placing of a £750,000 order for three civil Wessex helicopters. Based on the RAF's HC Mk.2, the Wessex Mk.60 was to be used in conjunction

with British Petroleum (BP) and Burmah Oil companies, which had recently announced the start of oil and gas exploration work in the North Sea. This initial order was soon increased to five.

The prototype, reusing the company B-class registration G-17-1, flew on 21 July 1965. The aircraft was largely the same as the HC Mk.2 and HU Mk.5 military variants, and were powered by a pair of civil-certified 1,352shp Rolls-Royce Gnome H.1200 Mk.660 engines. These engines were to the same basic build standard as those fitted to the Vertol 107 which had themselves been approved in the Transport Category as far back as August 1963. The all-important coupling gearbox was cleared for civil use in September and the first aircraft, now reregistered as G-ASWI, received ARB approval the following month. The cabin was fitted out for 16 passengers in basic seating that could be folded to allow a freight load to be carried instead.

The first of the initial five aircraft entered service with Bristow in support of the BP oil rigs in the North Sea, beginning operations from Tetney heliport near Grimsby in October the same year, followed by North Denes near Great Yarmouth. With the increase in gas and oil exploration in the North Sea and the Wessex proving to be very capable, a further 12 aircraft were ordered by Bristow in June the following year. Production would continue until 1972, with

one former Ghanaian Mk.53 being converted later by Bristow at Redhill.

Ocean Prince

During the night of 5/6 March 1968, the semi-submersible Burmah Oil drilling barge *Ocean Prince*, which had hit the headlines nearly 18 months earlier for being the first rig to discover deposits of oil in the British sector of the North Sea, found itself being battered by a fierce storm 100 miles off the Lincolnshire coast. Waves up to 50ft were pounding the structure, parts of which were beginning to fall into the freezing waters, threatening the lives of the 45 men on board. Despite winds gusting up to 90kt, Captain Bob Balls flew his Wessex Mk.60 from Scarborough heliport solo out to the stricken rig. Two loads of workers were flown from the *Ocean Prince* to the rig Constellation some 20 miles away and the third had just been plucked to safety when the landing platform collapsed into the sea. A few hours later the remains of the rig disappeared beneath the waves. For his gallantry in the rescue, Bob Balls was awarded the MBE.

A year later, on 16 April 1969, G-AWXX became the 100th helicopter to be delivered to the Bristow company and, shortly afterwards on 8 June, embarked on a record-breaking long-distance delivery flight to Australia. Leaving Gatwick Airport, 'XX arrived at Broome three weeks later on 29 June after completing the 11,184-mile route. From there it then went on to Port Samson for use in oil exploration work with the Burmah Oil Company of Australia.

Accidents

The Wessex Mk.60's reputation was, however, to be tarnished by two crashes which occurred during its service. The first happened on 9 September 1972 when G-ATCA lost control in a low hover and crashed at Rhoose, Cardiff, being burnt out in the ensuing fire. The crew of two escaped with injuries. It was to be a much more serious accident, however, that would seal the type's fate. On 13 August 1981, G-ASWI, the original Westland company demonstrator now owned by Bristow, was en route from the Leman gas field in the North Sea to a landing site at Bacton with 11 passengers on board. Suddenly, 15 miles offshore, the pilot issued a Mayday call, stating that he was ditching after engine failure. Nothing further was heard. An RAF Sea King scrambled from Coltishall located some of the wreckage just a quarter of an hour

later. Of the two crew and 11 passengers, there were no survivors.

This final accident was to effectively signal the end of operations by Bristow of the Mk.60. The company's remaining ten airframes were immediately grounded. While some were sold to Uruguay, many of the remaining aircraft were returned to Westlands at Weston-super-Mare, where they languished in storage.

Logging and film work

In 1987, a few Mk.60s were modified to look like USMC H-34 Choctaws for the Stanley Kubrick Vietnam war film *Full Metal Jacket*, which was filmed in the UK.

Some ex-Bristow Mk.60s were also bought by Flight Services International at Thruxton, Helicopter Hire, Sykes and Glosair, but in such small numbers the aircraft proved to be expensive to run and their use was therefore short-lived. Today, only a few of the 20 aircraft built remain in museums such as the International Helicopter Museum at Weston-super-Mare.

BELOW Following the withdrawal of the Mk.60 from service after the fatal crashes, most examples ended up in storage at Westland's Weston-super-Mare factory.
(Leonardo Helicopters)

Chapter Seven

Other operators

In stark contrast to its predecessors, the WS-51 and the WS-55 Whirlwind, commercial and foreign military export success was to elude the Wessex. Though once the re-engined Wessex was technologically much more advanced than any offering from other manufacturers, by the time that the British military priority orders had been completed, the Americans had caught up and the gas turbine was now being fitted to their own designs on a much larger and cheaper scale.

OPPOSITE **The first of the RAN Wessex HAS Mk.31s snort into life at Yeovil prior to delivery, 30 August 1962.** *(Leonardo Helicopters)*

Although a very small number of foreign export variants were designed and built, the only major military contract to be placed with Westland for the Wessex outside the UK came from the Royal Australian Navy (RAN). A number were also put to use exclusively with some of the British test and evaluation establishments where they provided many years of sterling service in helping not only to improve the capabilities and safe operation of the British variants, but also helped to devise new technologies that would go on to feature in some of the helicopters in use today.

HAS Mk.31 and 31B: Royal Australian Navy

Twenty-seven Wessex were built specifically for the RAN and designated initially as the HAS Mk.31. These were basically the same as the Royal Navy's HAS Mk.1 variants but were fitted with the more powerful Gazelle Mk.162 engine. The first aircraft, WA200, was officially handed over to the RAN at Yeovil on 30 August 1962 and deliveries to Australia began shortly thereafter.

Four RAN air squadrons were equipped with the aircraft 723, 725, 816 and 817, embarking in the carriers HMAS *Melbourne* and HMAS

ABOVE Australian troops conducting 'rapelling' from a Wessex HAS Mk.31B N7-218 ('828') of 817 RANAS, August 1985. *(via Jeff Chartier)*

BELOW RAN Wessex HAS Mk.31Bs at RANAS Nowra. *(via Jeff Chartier)*

Sydney, as well as the support ships HMAS Stalwart, Tobruk and Success.

In line with the upgrading of some of the RN's HAS Mk.1 aircraft to HAS Mk.3, the 26 surviving HAS Mk.31 airframes were also put through a conversion programme to bring them up to the new HAS Mk.31B configuration. This saw them being fitted with the same Gazelle Mk.165 engine as their British counterparts, as well as receiving new radar, improved TACAN navigational and ultra high frequency (UHF) communications systems.

On Christmas Day 1974, Cyclone Tracy hit the Darwin area of the Northern Territories causing huge devastation. Seven Wessex of 723 Squadron were quickly put into action to provide support to the humanitarian mission, codenamed Operation Navy Help, lifting much-needed electrical generators and helping to repair downed overhead power lines. The operation lasted for 17 days, during which the aircraft flew over 300 hours, moved almost 8,000 people and lifted over a million kilograms of vital stores and equipment.

With the introduction of the much more capable Sea King HAS Mk.50 aircraft, the Wessex were gradually relegated to the utility role in the mid-1970s. Finally, in 1989, the type was withdrawn

ABOVE Wessex Mk.52 WA227 ('588') of the Iraqi Air Force during test flying at Yeovil. *(Leonardo Helicopters)*

BELOW The cabin of the Iraqi Air Force Mk.52. *(Leonardo Helicopters)*

ABOVE **Ghanaian Wessex Mk.53 G631.** *(Author's collection)*

from service, happily with several examples finding their way into aviation museums.

Foreign orders

Only the RAN operated export versions of the Gazelle-powered aircraft. Modified versions of the Gnome-powered Wessex were, however, sold to several other foreign countries, albeit in small numbers. The Mk.52 was ordered by the Iraqi Air Force while the Mk.53 was supplied to the Ghanaian Air Force and the Mk.54 to the Royal Brunei Air Force. Bangladesh was presented with two ex-RN HU Mk.5s – XT452 and XT478 – redesignated as Mk.5A, by the British government for humanitarian duties at a reported cost of £1 million.

But by far the most numerous foreign operator of the Wessex was Uruguay. Former Ghanaian Mk.53s and Brunei Mk.54s were sold to Uruguay, which would later take on retired HC Mk.2s direct from 28 (AC) Squadron at Hong Kong, plus examples shipped out from the UK, together with some ex-Bristow Mk.60s.

LEFT **Formerly RAF Wessex HC Mk.2 XR505, '081' of the Uruguayan Navy lands aboard the USS** *Oak Hill* **in the Atlantic while conducting combined amphibious operations with the US Navy, 9 July 2009.** *(US DoD)*

RIGHT **Wessex HU Mk.5 XT768 was used by Westland for icing trials and is seen here with a special camera mounted on top of the MRH which could film the build-up of ice on each rotor blade in flight.** *(Leonardo Helicopters)*

Trials aircraft

Many Wessex of various marks were used, either permanently or on loan, by both the Royal Aircraft Establishments at Farnborough and Bedford and by the A&AEE at Boscombe Down throughout the service life of the aircraft. As well as carrying out the trials necessary to underpin the development and safe use of the aircraft in service, valuable research work was also undertaken, including studies into main rotor blade icing and glass cockpit trials which would later be used on aircraft such as the Merlin.

Aerial logging

After being retired from service, eight ex-RAF HC Mk.2s and HU Mk.5Cs subsequently found their way to New Zealand where they were placed on the civil register to undertake aerial logging work. During one such sortie in February 2001, the former XS509 (now ZK-HVK) crashed into a valley after engine failure, killing the pilot. The ensuing investigation led to the New Zealand CAA eventually rescinding the type's certificate of airworthiness due to 'irregularities' in its operation.

ABOVE Royal Aircraft Establishment Wessex HU Mk.5 XT762. *(Author's collection)*

RIGHT Wessex HU Mk.5 XS509 of the Empire Test Pilots' School, Boscombe Down, seen here visiting RNAY Fleetlands. *(RNAY Fleetlands)*

LEFT Between April and November 1974, four 72 Squadron Wessex HC Mk.2s were loaned to the Sultanate of Muscat and Oman Air Force to assist with the construction of the defensive Hornbeam Line near the Omani–Yemeni border during the Dhofari Campaign, one such example being XR511. The aircraft retained their RAF serials but adopted Omani roundels and a Light Stone/Dark Earth/black camouflage. *(Sid Pass)*

Chapter Eight

Anatomy of the Wessex

Operating in some of the most inhospitable environments in the world, helicopters intended for operations from ships at sea have to be designed to be rugged and dependable. The Wessex was both. But what made it stand out from the rest was its incredible versatility, which allowed it to undertake much more than its original anti-submarine role.

OPPOSITE A Wessex will live again! Former 771 NAS Wessex HU Mk.5 XT761 (foreground) being restored to fly at Crewkerne, Somerset, in 2017, with XT771 awaiting similar treatment. _(Author)_

Fuselage

The Wessex fuselage was made from four major structural sections: the nose, the cabin (including rear compartment), the tailcone and the tail pylon. All four of these were of semi-monocoque light alloy construction.

Nose structure

Often, the easiest identifying feature of the Wessex variants was the differing nose profile brought about by the changes in engines throughout its life: the HAS Mk.1, HAS Mk.3, HAS Mk.31 and Mk.31B with the Napier Gazelle and the HC Mk.2, HCC Mk.4 and HU Mk.5 with the Rolls-Royce Gnome.

The upper nose structure was divided into two compartments by a longitudinal bulkhead running along the aircraft's centreline. Within the port (left) side compartment was the radio equipment, while in the starboard (right) side was the aircraft's electrical equipment.

The lower nose structure was effectively the

engine compartment. An air intake door, hinged at its upper end, was fitted at the front, while at the rear of the compartment was the titanium firewall bulkhead. On the HAS Mk.1 and HAS Mk.3, this took the form of a dome-shaped door with optional air intake guards while on the Gnome-powered variants this was later changed to a chin-type door with integral anti-icing and particle separator ducting.

Small doors on either side of the Gazelle-powered aircraft, hinged on their lower edges, had double purposes: to allow access to the engine but also, by virtue of inbuilt steps, to gain access to the radio and electrical compartments. For the other variants, however, larger rectangular access doors gave access to the engines only.

A 'fireproof' zone was created at the rear of the engine compartment by curved titanium panels that fitted either side of the engine.

On the Gnome-powered variants, scoops under the nose door, and side access doors provided cooling air to both of the compressor

BELOW The basic construction of a Wessex fuselage. *(AP101C-0105)*

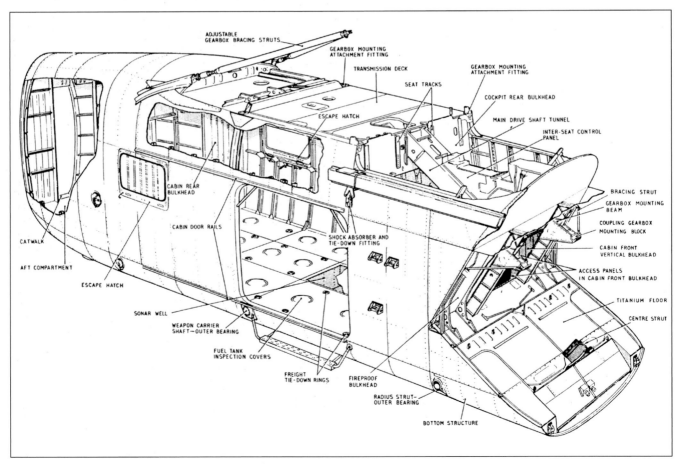

LEFT LEFT Frontal view of Wessex HAS Mk.1 XS863 ('304/R') preserved at IWM Duxford, showing the original nose intake. *(Author)*

ABOVE View of Wessex HAS Mk.3 XP142 with the electrical compartment, engine air intake and servicing platforms open. *(Author)*

BELOW Nose access doors and panels open on Wessex HU Mk.5 XT765. *(Author)*

ABOVE Starboard nose electrical compartment on a Wessex HAS Mk.3. *(Author)*

LEFT Port nose electrical compartment on a Wessex HAS Mk.3. Some of the equipment has been removed from their mounting trays. *(Author)*

BELOW LEFT Air intake on the port side of the nose feeding cooling air to the Gnome engine coupling gearbox of a Wessex HU Mk.5. *(Author)*

BELOW Coupling gearbox oil cooler matrix and exhaust viewed through the starboard side. *(Author)*

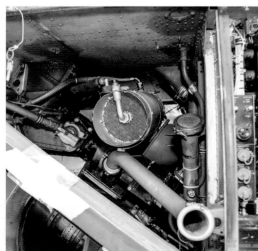

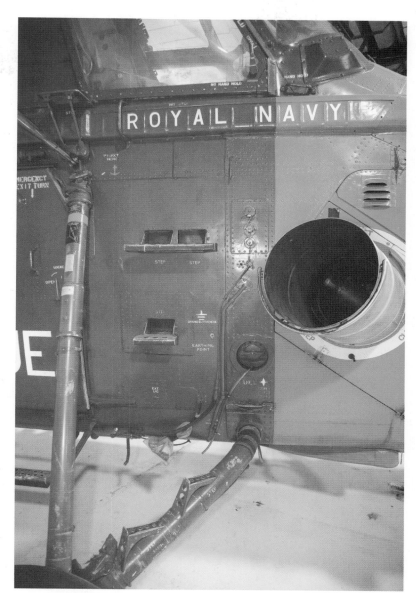

RIGHT Footsteps built into the undercarriage strut and fuselage side allow access to the cockpit. *(Author)*

and turbine sections. A separate scoop was installed on the port side electrical bay door for the coupling gearbox oil cooler fan, which exhausted through a circular hole on the starboard side door.

Cockpit

Situated high above the forward section of the fuselage immediately above the forward end of the cabin and just aft of the nose section, was the cockpit. Gaining access required a degree of 'mountaineering' effort by the pilot. First, a step was fitted on each of the main oleo fixed struts; from here, a series of dual foot-/handholds were built into the side of the fuselage on either side; finally, a set of three handholds were provided around the canopy structure.

A one-piece canopy structure comprising five front windscreens and six overhead glazings enclosed the cockpit. Each panel could be replaced individually or the whole assembly removed and replaced as a single unit. Reinforced areas on the upper structure of the canopy allowed personnel to stand on them to gain access to the main rotor head.

Having reached the top of this veritable climbing frame, the large glazed window panels on either side, which doubled as access doors and which could be jettisoned in an emergency, were slid open and, using the handholds above, the pilots could then swing themselves into the cockpit seat.

Windscreen wipers

Each pilot had their own independent windscreen wiper. These were hydraulically powered by electrically driven pumps mounted on the cockpit floor and could be selected for normal and fast speeds using a rotary switch on the overhead console. When switched off, the wiper blades were automatically returned to a parked position.

RIGHT Cockpit canopy assembly, windscreens and wipers. *(Author)*

THE WINDSCREEN WIPER GENIE

The Wessex's windscreen wiper system was viewed fondly by some as a most fabulous and complex arrangement as one former pilot recalls:

This was a development from the Whirlwind, where all systems were controlled by a doll, for a doll it was, as there were numerous 'dolls' eyes' that winked at you from under the Whirlwind instrument panel whenever said 'doll' had mischief in mind.

Clearly, this would not do for the more macho Wessex, so a genie was installed during the build at Yeovil. This genie allowed electricity to be made from the noise produced by the engines through their friends, the inverters. They certainly were 'in'-verters as very little electricity was allowed out to the rest of the aircraft, but that is another story.

Should the pilot be wilful enough to switch on the windscreen wipers, a lot could – and usually did – happen.

The principal area of activity surrounded the electromechanical-hydro mechanism that lived on the floor of the cockpit. The first indication of action was the leaking of copious amounts of hydraulic fluid on to the

floor under the second pilot's feet, thus converting their non-slip footwear to hi-slip. What hydraulic fluid remained was pumped up to the next device, situated close by the windscreen. It was here that much more activity was enabled by the genie, with even more mischief in mind.

At first, all appeared well. The rain was on the screen, the wiper blade wiped, and then . . . any oil that had found its way on the outside of the windscreen would be promptly wiped, mixed with the rainwater, thus rendering the windscreen opaque.

Any deliberations on their now non-existent forward view by our, now bemused, aviator was rendered redundant by the next phase of the operation as the wiper blade, having done its work, would depart the aircraft, whereupon it could – and often did – impact with either a main or tail rotor blade. In this case, the ensuing vibration would take one's mind off not being able to see anything ahead.

If some, or any, of the above was not enough, the by now fed up electromechanical-hydro device would promptly overheat and emit an evil smell . . . or just catch fire.

Windscreen de-icing

On the HU Mk.5, the three separate Triplex 'Hyvis' windscreen panels were also electrically heated to provide a de-icing function.

Crew seats

Both cockpit seats were mounted on to rails on the inclined bulkhead on which they could be raised and lowered. The seat pans were hinged so that they could be folded up or tilted forward to allow access to the rear cabin. In the HCC Mk.4, removal of the seat cushion would allow a seat-type or back-type parachute pack to be carried.

Instrument panel and cockpit lighting

The main instrument panel on all Wessex variants was divided into three separate units: centre, right (first pilot) and left (second pilot), and spanned the width of the cockpit beneath the windscreen, tilted forward at an angle of 23° from the vertical. A black-painted lighting screen shroud was fitted over the top to prevent light from any of the illuminated instruments from

ABOVE The cockpit of a Wessex HU Mk.5. *(Author)*

LEFT Cockpit of Wessex HCC Mk.4 XV733 showing the moving map assembly on the cockpit coaming and the much more comfortable seat upholstery. *(Author)*

LEFT Wessex HU Mk.5 left-hand instrument panel. (*Author*)

1 Compass
2 Air speed indicator
3 Radio altimeter
4 Turn and slip indicator
5 Compass correction card
6 Standby artificial horizon
7 Artificial horizon
8 Vertical rate of climb/ descent
9 Barometric altimeter
10 ASI correction card
11 Instrument lighting control

LEFT Wessex HU Mk.5 right-hand instrument panel. (*Author*)

1 Compass
2 Air speed indicator
3 Radio altimeter
4 Turn and slip indicator
5 Standby artificial horizon
6 Artificial horizon
7 Vertical rate of climb/ descent
8 Barometric altimeter
9 Cargo release light
10 Cockpit light control
11 Hover meter
12 Generator load ammeter
13 Sliding window jettison handle

ABOVE Wessex HU Mk.5 centre instrument panel. *(Author)*

1 Port engine oil temperature

2 Starboard engine oil temperature

3 Port engine oil pressure

4 Starboard engine oil pressure

5 Clock (missing)

6 Coupling gearbox oil pressure

7 Coupling gearbox oil temperature

8 MRGB oil pressure

9 MRGB oil temperature

10 Primary hydraulic system pressure

11 Secondary hydraulic system pressure

12 Flare master switch

13 Cockpit light

14 Centralised warning panel

15 Engine fire extinguisher buttons

16 Port fuel tank air pressure

17 Port fuel contents

18 Starboard fuel tank contents

19 Starboard fuel tank air pressure

20 Main rotor RPM

21 Main rotor torquemeter

22 Port engine fuel flow meter

23 Starboard engine fuel flow meter

24 Fuel emergency jettison switch (guarded)

25 Port engine power turbine temperature

26 Starboard engine power turbine temperature

27 Port engine gas turbine rpm

28 Starboard engine gas turbine rpm

29 Fuel cross-feed controls

30 Standby AC power switch

31 Generator switches

32 Master battery switch

LEFT Wessex HU Mk.5 overhead console.
(Author)

1 Cockpit light
2 Map stowage
3 Lighting control panel
4 Overhead blind
5 External light controls
6 Windscreen wiper and heat switches
7 Electrical system switches
8 IFF controller
9 UHF/VHF radio controller
10 HF radio
11 Telebrief controller
12 Doppler controller
13 UHF radio controller
14 Homing controller
15 UHF/VHF radio controller
16 Rotor brake handle
17 Rotor brake system gauge
18 Outside air temperature gauge

being reflected in the windscreen and also to reduce the amount of ambient light to allow the lit instruments to be seen in daylight.

Working from left to right, the second pilot's panel featured a compass repeater, air speed indicator (ASI), radio altimeter (RadAlt), barometric altimeter (BarAlt), artificial horizon, attitude indicator and rate of climb indicator. The artificial horizon was electrically operated and contained a gyro, while the altimeters, ASI and rate of climb indicators were all operated by low-pressure air from the pitot-static system.

The centre panel contained all of the transmission and engine instrumentation: engine oil pressure and both oil and temperature pressure gauges for the transmission and hydraulic systems were mounted in a double row to the left, fitted in a such a way as to have the needles pointing vertically upwards when everything was operating within normal ranges. Doing this was a simple and effective way of making any degraded system stand out from the others and was easier for the pilots to detect. For the twin-engined variants, each had its own set of instruments, together with a coupling gearbox indication.

In the middle of the centre panel was the centralised warning panel (CWP). Beneath the CWP were the fuel contents indicators.

On the right of the centre panel were the rotor tachometer and torquemeter. Beneath these were the fuel flow indicators, while at the bottom was the gas generator tachometer indicator (two for the Gnome-powered aircraft).

On the right-hand side of the cockpit was the pilot's panel, identical to the second pilot's with the one exception of the inclusion of a UHF radio homing indicator.

Overhead console

Depending on the variant, the overhead console featured controls for the Doppler and compass control units, radios, lighting, windscreen wiper and hoist.

To reduce glare entering the cockpit from the upper window assemblies, concertina-type nylon blinds were fitted which could be drawn forward, guided along wires threaded through eyelets in the blinds and secured in position with straps and press-stud fasteners.

On the rear bulkhead behind the right-hand

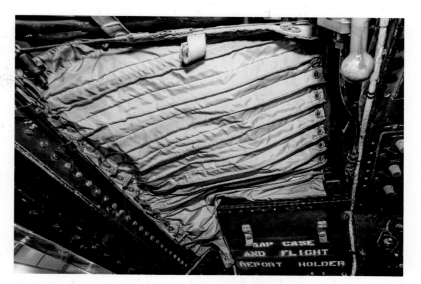

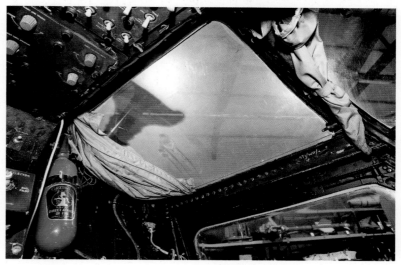

seat was a map stowage box. For the HCC Mk.4 this was later converted to accommodate a personal locator beacon.

Interseat console

The interseat console differed somewhat depending on the aircraft variant and role fit. A multitude of equipment could be installed here, ranging from autopilot and hover controls, UHF radio controller, high-pressure (HP) and low-pressure (LP) fuel cock controls, compass control unit, autopilot control unit, through to engine drive selection and a single push button for engine starting.

On the Gnome-engined aircraft, a separate switch selected which of the two engines was to be started before this button would be pressed, and switches and indicators for

TOP Overhead anti-glare blind. *(Author)*

ABOVE Overhead anti-glare blind in retracted position. *(Author)*

the engine fuel computers were included. The speed select levers (SSLs) were connected to the engine control box below the cockpit and from there to the engine automatic fuel computers in the nose.

To the right of the main interseat console were the controls for operating the landing lamp, while to the left were the switches and indicators for the nose air intake door anti-icing system.

Pitot-static system

To provide air pressure for the ASI and BarAlt cockpit instruments, the Wessex had two independent pitot pressure heads mounted at the end of light alloy tubes protruding through the cabin roof and angled to face into the airflow – the starboard side feeding the first pilot's instruments and the port supplying the second pilot's. The heads were electrically heated to prevent the build-up of ice in cold weather conditions. Flexible hoses then directed the air down and into a manifold at the rear of the instrument panel and then into the instruments themselves. The HCC Mk.4 differed from all other marks in having two such pressure heads mounted on the starboard side.

Cabin

The main cabin measured 13ft 6in long, 5ft 3in wide and 5ft 10in in height, giving an overall capacity of 410cu ft.

Troop seating

In the trooping role, the Wessex could be fitted with a series of basic troop seats comprised of metal tubular frames with fabric covering. The fabric of the seat sections were supported and tensioned by lengths of nylon cord tied through eyelets and laced around the tubes.

The tubular legs, welded to form triangular assemblies, were secured to the cabin floor by recessed spring-loaded press studs. By releasing these studs to disengage the seat legs from the floor, the seat pans could be quickly folded up to lie flat against the cabin sides

RIGHT Port side cabin windows on a Wessex HU Mk.5. Both could be jettisoned in an emergency by turning the striped handles. (Author)

LEFT Wessex HU Mk.5 armament selector panel to the right of the right-hand seat position. (Author)
1 Flare controls
2 Upper RP controls
3 Lower RP controls
4 Gun control switch

BELOW The double pitot arrangement on Wessex HCC Mk.4 XV733. All other Wessex variants had just the uppermost of these two masts. (Author)

ABOVE Wessex HU Mk.5 cabin looking aft. The troop seating on the starboard side aft of the cabin door is in the folded position. *(Author)*

ABOVE RIGHT View of the cabin looking forward. Steps are built into the forward bulkhead to aid access to/from the cockpit. *(Author)*

RIGHT View looking up to the cockpit with the right-hand cockpit seat in the folded position. The driveshaft from the coupling gearbox to the MRGB runs through the channel section between the two seats. *(Author)*

BELOW Bars with fluorescent-painted cones orientated to effectively point the way to the escape routes run around the cabin. *(Author)*

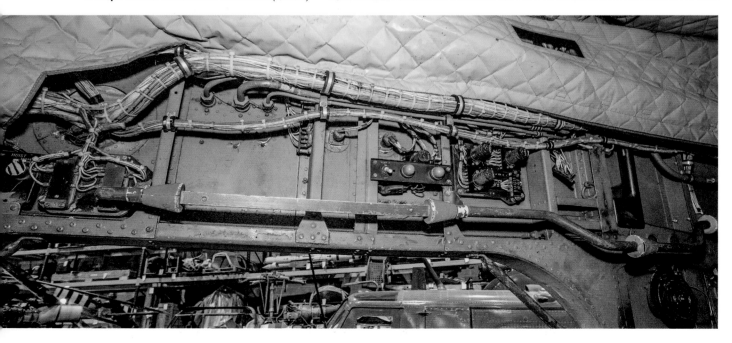

LEFT The HCC Mk.4 featured an additional window on the port side of the cabin and the larger windows of the RN variants. *(Author)*

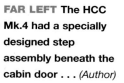

FAR LEFT The HCC Mk.4 had a specially designed step assembly beneath the cabin door . . . *(Author)*

LEFT . . . which could be manually folded for flight. *(Author)*

BELOW The later cabin configuration and trim of the HCC Mk.4. The two flotation canisters are seen at left, normally fitted to the mainwheels. *(Author)*

when not in use. The fabric which formed the backs to the seats was held taut vertically by being clipped to a horizontal bar secured by open-jawed fittings, pip pins and spring-loaded retaining balls to brackets on the cabin walls. These quick-release mechanisms allowed the bar to be quickly pulled out to lower the fabric backs and give clear access to the emergency exit windows and hatches behind them.

In the HC Mk.2, the cabin was capable of carrying up to 16 seated individuals: a bank of six forward on the port side and three aft,

BELOW A later feature of the HCC Mk.4 VVIP interior was a drinks and cutlery cabinet in between the two forward seats. Note that there was no access between cabin and cockpit. *(Author)*

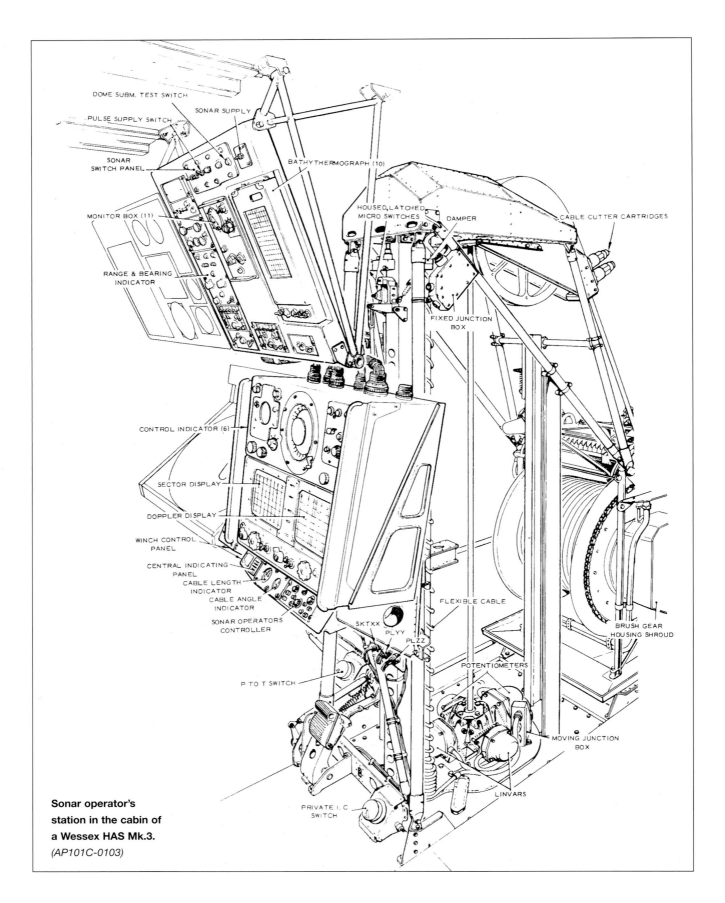

DOME SUBM. TEST SWITCH

PULSE SUPPLY SWITCH

SONAR SUPPLY

SONAR SWITCH PANEL

BATHYTHERMOGRAPH (10)

MONITOR BOX (11)

HOUSED, LATCHED MICRO SWITCHES

DAMPER

CABLE CUTTER CARTRIDGES

RANGE & BEARING INDICATOR

FIXED JUNCTION BOX

CONTROL INDICATOR (6)

SECTOR DISPLAY

DOPPLER DISPLAY

WINCH CONTROL PANEL

CENTRAL INDICATING PANEL

CABLE LENGTH INDICATOR

CABLE ANGLE INDICATOR

SONAR OPERATORS CONTROLLER

SKTXX

PLYY

PLZZ

FLEXIBLE CABLE

BRUSH GEAR HOUSING SHROUD

POTENTIOMETERS

P TO T SWITCH

MOVING JUNCTION BOX

LINVARS

PRIVATE I.C SWITCH

**Sonar operator's
station in the cabin of
a Wessex HAS Mk.3.**
(AP101C-0103)

two on the starboard side forward of the cabin door, and five aft of the cabin door, all facing inboard.

For the HU Mk.5, up to 13 seated troops could be accommodated. The difference from the HC Mk.2 was on the port side, immediately aft of the forward bulkhead, where the large box-like fairing on the floor covering the autopilot was used as the three-man seat. A further bank of six trooping seats could be fitted aft of these. All such troop seats had their own airliner-type single lapstrap.

Cabin role fits

ASW configuration

For the ASW variants, a seat was provided aft of the respective stations for the Observer and the Sonar Operator. In addition, an instructor seat could also be fitted behind the latter. The seats had electrical connectors to allow heated aircrew clothing to be used.

Three instrument panels are provided at the rear stations. The left-hand (Observer) and right-hand (Sonar Operator) panels mounted above are both angled downwards. The Observer panel contains a Doppler control unit, ASI, BarAlt, ground speed and drift indicator, and a compass master indicator. The Sonar Operator panel features a bathythermograph recorder, intercom box, radio station box, range and bearing controller, HF radio control unit and transponder controls.

The sonar control panel (in front of the Sonar Operator) is angled slightly upwards and houses the sonar controller, cable angle and cable out indicators, sector and Doppler displays.

To the left of the sonar control panel and in front of the Observer's position is the indicator azimuth range display unit. A large cathode ray tube unit projected the primary and secondary radar signals, sonar range and bearing markers on to an optical sub-unit mounted on an inclined plotting table. The circular plan position indicator (PPI) display on the unit presented heading markers as a succession of short lines, sonar bearing as a brightened trace to indicate the bearing of the target relative to compass north, and sonar range markers as 45° arcs within the bearing marker lines. Signals from other aircraft fitted with the ARI 5954

ABOVE The ASW configuration of the Wessex HAS Mk.3. At the end of the type's service, most of the equipment was robbed to fit to the Sea King, leaving the exhibits like this one (XM328) at the International Helicopter Museum devoid of many of the components. *(Author)*

transponders up to 20 miles away could also be displayed during a co-ordinated attack.

Paratrooping

A master switch which determines who is in control of the hoist is also used in conjunction with a role switch to provide the option of using some of the same switches for a paratrooping role. With the master switch set to 'Pilot' and the role switch set to 'Troop', a set of green and red lamps above the inside of the cabin door can be operated, together with a warning klaxon horn, to signal to troops in the cabin when to commence their jump.

Stretchers

Provision was also made for carriage of stretchers to ferry injured and sick personnel from the battlefield. Mounted to special vertical stanchions using the same attachment brackets for the troop seats and a series of straps tensioned between the cabin roof and floor, three stretchers could be

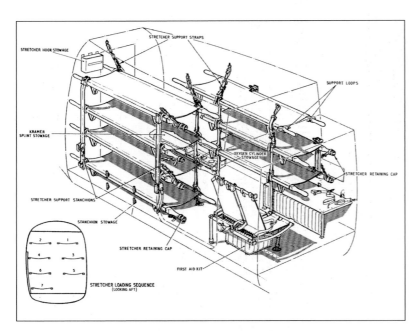

ABOVE Cabin stretcher configuration in the medical evacuation role. *(AP101C-0105)*

ABOVE RIGHT View inside the tailcone of Wessex HAS Mk.3 XP142 showing the tail rotor driveshaft running along the top and maintenance walkway along the bottom. Tail rotor control rods can be seen along the starboard side. *(Author)*

mounted on the port side, one above the other, and four on the starboard side. In this medical evacuation role, the starboard two-man seat was retained for the medical attendant.

Medical equipment

A range of medical equipment could be carried, including a Kramer Splint, stowage for up to eight medical oxygen bottles, a first-aid kit, a Neil Robertson stretcher for use with the external hoist for loading and unloading casualties while the aircraft was in the hover, and up to four Stokes litters.

Sea tray

When carrying out SAR operations or wet winching drills, large quantities of sea water can become deposited within the cabin. This highly corrosive salt water can then find its way into the aircraft structure and wreak havoc with the aluminium and magnesium alloy skins.

To prevent this from happening, aircraft nominated for these types of operational role are fitted with a sea tray: a waterproof floor made from Marglass cloth and coated in PVC. This sits on top of the existing cabin floor and specially moulded reinforced elements protect it from being punctured by protruding items; 9in high walls around its edge provide a barrier to prevent water ingress and the whole assembly is secured to the structure by press studs and a metal plate at the cargo door aperture.

Tail unit

The tail unit comprises three main sections: the tailcone, the tail pylon and the horizontal stabiliser.

Tailcone

The tailcone structure is made up of six channel section frames and two bulkheads – fore and aft – all given additional strength by longitudinal stringers and intercostals. Initially, these intercostals and outer skins were of magnesium alloy. However, these became severely affected by corrosion in service and eventually most components were replaced with aluminium alloy alternatives. A narrow aluminium alloy honeycomb sandwich 'catwalk' is installed along the bottom of the inside of the unit to allow maintenance personnel to gain access.

At the rear of the tailcone was the tail fold casting which allowed the tail pylon to be unlocked by manually withdrawing a vertical pin using an inbuilt ratchet mechanism. It could then be swung through almost 90° to face aft along the port side of the tail for stowage on board ship.

Running down the external spine of the tailcone are a series of eight square patches of non-slip painted areas that correspond with the internal frames, nominated as reinforced points on which maintenance personnel could safely walk without causing any damage. Footsteps built into the rear frame of the tailcone, visible when the tail pylon is folded, and an external handhold on the starboard side, allowed personnel to climb up to reach the tail rotor.

Tail pylon

The tail pylon is attached to the tailcone by hinge castings, allowing it to be folded. Installed within the lower section, and accessible through removable panels, is the intermediate gearbox with the tail rotor driveshaft running up through the pylon to the tail rotor gearbox mounted at the upper end. The pylon is aerofoil-shaped, so that in forward flight the airflow over it allows lift to be generated and thus helps to offload the tail rotor in countering the torque of the main rotor.

Horizontal stabiliser

A 5ft 8in horizontal stabiliser of symmetrical aerofoil section is fitted on the forward beam of the tail pylon to assist with longitudinal stability in forward flight. Made with two channel section aluminium alloy spars and alloy skin, the port side is strengthened to form a footstep allowing maintenance personnel to use it to gain access to higher parts such as the tail rotor and tail rotor gearbox areas. The rear spar attaches to two lugs while a turnbuckle connects the front spar to the pylon, allowing for adjustment of the incidence of the stabiliser.

Sonar equipment

In the ASW role, the main cabin of the Wessex HAS variants was dominated by the sonar equipment and its associated winching gear.

Type 194

The Type 194 'searchlight' sonar was a British version of the American AQS-4 sonar and had earlier been fitted to the Whirlwind HAS Mk.7. It had a 21° scan beam with a range of up to 3,000yd and could reach to a depth of 50ft.

The sonar worked by sending pulses of acoustic energy through a submersible transducer body lowered on the end of a cable from the aircraft into the water. This sonar submersible unit was held securely within a rudimentary-looking tubular framework structure within the cabin when stowed. In much the same way as radar works above the surface,

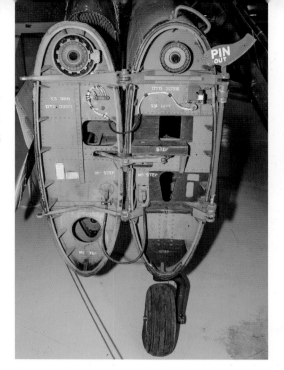

LEFT View of the tail pylon (left) and tailcone fold joint showing the integral footsteps, disconnect coupling and locking mechanism. *(Author)*

BELOW Tail pylon assembly. *(AP101C-0101)*

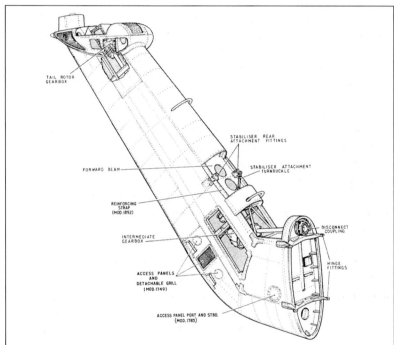

LEFT Horizontal stabiliser. *(Author)*

LEFT Westland Wessex HAS Mk.3.

(Mike Badrocke)

1 Tail navigation lights
2 Anti-collision light
3 Cooling air grilles
4 Tail rotor gearbox fairing
5 Final drive right-angle gearbox
6 Tail rotor hub mechanism
7 Blade pitch angle control linkage
8 Four-bladed tail rotor
9 Handgrip
10 Tail rotor drive shaft
11 Tail pylon construction
12 Fixed horizontal tailplane construction
13 Ground handling grips
14 Cooling air grilles
15 Bevel drive gearbox
16 Port tailplane
17 Folding tail pylon hinge joint
18 Tail pylon latching mechanism
19 Tailwheel shock absorber strut
20 Castoring tailwheel
21 Hinged axle beam
22 Mooring ring
23 Aerial mast
24 HF aerial cable
25 Rotor blade trailing edge rib construction
26 Tip fairing
27 Blade tracking weight
28 Blade balance weights
29 D-section aluminium blade spar
30 Transponder aerial
31 Tailcone frame and stringer construction
32 Tail rotor control cables
33 Tail rotor transmission shaft
34 Upper IFF aerial
35 UHF aerial
36 Tailcone/fuselage joint frame
37 Equipment bay bulkhead
38 Dorsal radome
39 Search radar scanner
40 Radome mounting structure
41 Port side cabin heater
42 Electrical system equipment
43 Fuel delivery piping
44 Rear fuel tank group filler cap
45 Pressure refuelling connection
46 Mk 46 torpedo
47 External fuel tank, capacity 454 litres (100 Imp gal)
48 External cable ducting
49 Aft crash-proof fuel cells; total fuel capacity 1,209 litres (266 Imp gal)
50 Cabin window/escape hatch
51 Cabin rear bulkhead
52 Curtained aperture to equipment bay
53 Vent piping
54 Oil cooler air exit louvres
55 Rotor head rear aerodynamic fairing
56 Oil cooler
57 Rear fairing access panels
58 Cabin heating ducting
59 Smoke marker stowage
60 Marker launch tube cover
61 Cabin floor panelling
62 External stores carrier
63 Stores pylon fixing
64 Dipping sonar
65 Floor beam construction
66 Cabin door
67 Seat mounting rails
68 Tactical navigator and sonar operator seats
69 Instrument consoles
70 Rescue hoist/winch
71 Gearbox mounting deck

72 Gearbox support struts
73 Rotor brake
74 Oil cooler fan
75 Gearbox deck access panels
76 Rotor head servo control units
77 Blade pitch control linkage
78 Torque scissor links
79 Blade drag damper
80 Hydraulic oil reservoir
81 Rotor head mechanism
82 Four-blade main rotor
83 Blade root attachment joints
84 Cooling air grilles
85 Cockpit roof glazing
86 Overhead switch panel
87 Chart case
88 Servo motor switching control panel
89 Cockpit rear bulkhead
90 Pilot's seat
91 Sliding side window/entry hatch
92 Main landing gear leg strut attachment
93 Cabin door jettison lever
94 Sliding cabin door
95 Door latch
96 Shock absorber leg strut
97 Boarding step
98 Flotation bag inflation bottle
99 Starboard mainwheel
100 Flotation bag stowage
101 Mooring ring
102 Pivoted main axle beam
103 Step
104 Hydraulic brake pipe
105 Forward group of fuel cells
106 Fuel filler cap
107 Dipping sonar winch mechanism

108 Cockpit access steps
109 Bifurcated engine exhaust pipes, port and starboard
110 Cockpit floor level
111 External cable ducting
112 Handgrip
113 Rudder pedals
114 Instrument panel
115 Cyclic pitch control column
116 Collective pitch lever
117 Co-pilot's seat
118 Rotor brake control lever
119 Temperature gauge
120 Windscreen panels
121 Windscreen wipers
122 Instrument panel shroud
123 Windscreen de-icing fluid spray nozzle
124 Sloping cockpit front bulkhead
125 Engine/gearbox transmission shaft
126 Electrical equipment bay, radio and electronics bay on port side
127 Nose equipment bay access hatches
128 Cooling air scoop
129 Batteries (two)
130 Engine oil tank
131 Engine turbine section
132 Exhaust compartment firewalls
133 Ground power socket
134 Ventilating air intake
135 Starboard navigation light
136 Main axle beam mounting
137 Nose compartment framing
138 Engine bay access door
139 Throttle control linkage
140 Engine withdrawal rail

141 Engine mounting struts
142 Rolls-Royce (Napier) Gazelle 22 turboshaft engine
143 Engine bay ventilating air intake
144 Starter cartridge magazine
145 Hydraulic pump
146 Fire extinguisher bottles
147 Engine air inlet
148 Hinged nose cone access panel
149 Engine accessory equipment gearbox
150 Generator
151 Intake plenum
152 Retractable landing lamp
153 Lower IFF aerial

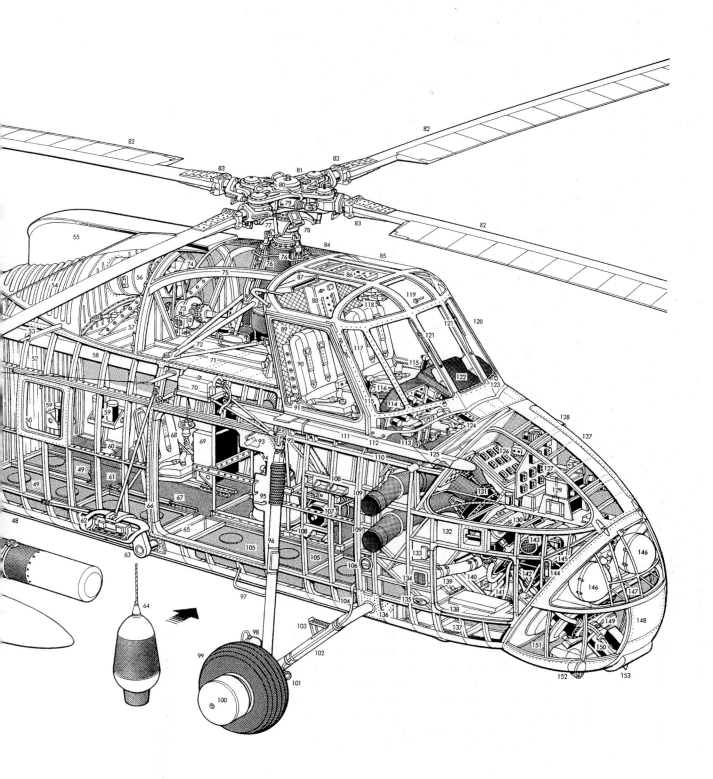

ABOVE The rear station of a Wessex HAS Mk.31 of the Royal Australian Navy. *(Leonardo Helicopters)*

RIGHT The Ryan sonar transducer, winch and winching gear in the HAS Mk.31. *(Leonardo Helicopters)*

ABOVE The original Type 194 sonar transducer head, often referred to as the 'searchlight' for obvious reasons. *(Author)*

the acoustic waves were reflected by solid objects underwater and the returning echoes sensed by the transducer.

Electronic units would then process the signals and the target range, vertical speed and bearing results would be displayed on two CRT screens mounted at the Observer's station, one displaying target range and vertical speed while the other showed target range and bearing. The audible acoustic 'ping' echo generated by the sonar was also fed into the aircrew's earphones. Some pilots were even known to become adept at detecting difficult contacts themselves.

Type 195

The Type 195 was designed specifically for helicopter use to detect submarines or other submerged objects. Like the Type 194 before it, the Type 195 was a simple dunking sonar; however, this new version featured a 90°-wide sector display with a linear time base presentation rather than a PPI-based sector and a Doppler display. The Doppler went from 35kt opening, through 0–35kt closing in three

LEFT Observer/winch controller stations (left), Type 195 sonar in the stowed position (centre) with winch gear (right) in a Wessex HAS Mk.3. *(Author)*

side-by-side vertical displays for left, centre and right within the sector being insonified. The time base on both the sector and Doppler display were matched. A contact was usually detected audibly first and then by looking for it on the sector and Doppler displays.

Unlike the 'searchlight'-shaped body of the earlier Type 194, the Type 195 on the HAS Mk.3 featured transducers mounted flush within a flat, rectangular body and a compass. A servo training system within the upper half of the transducer body could drive a motor to alter its bearing. This could be done manually or set to sweep through 90° sectors automatically, but the sonar would only be activated once the body reached a depth of 40ft.

Sonar winch

A 300ft flexible cable attaching the unit to the aircraft – and through which the electronic signals were sent and received – was routed up and around a pulley wheel at the top of the so-called 'pit-head' frame assembly (owing to it resembling the winch assembly of a coal mine) and then down on to a large hydraulically controlled drum at the forward end of the cabin. This drum, chain-driven from a reversible hydraulic motor, was controlled by a manually operated lever in between the Sonar Operator and Observer stations, winching the transducer up at a rate of 10ft per second and lowering it at 8ft per second. This rate was reduced to just 1.5ft per second when there was 15ft of cable between the sonar body and the aircraft for safety reasons. The drum could also be operated with a manual hand-winding gear in the event of hydraulic failure while the sonar was in use.

A foot-operated winch brake was fitted to prevent the submersible head from being lowered too fast and being either damaged or lost altogether. It would also engage automatically when approximately three turns of the cable remained on the drum as a safeguard to prevent it from over-running. A cable cutter was also incorporated to allow the cable to be severed in the event of an emergency with the sonar body still in the lowered position.

The clever part of the winch assembly was what was known as the travelling head. This was hooked to the locating ring at the top of the submersible head with the cable running

through its centre and moved on rollers up and down vertical guides with the submersible head. As the submersible head disappeared through the floor, the travelling head became unhooked and two restraining trap doors closed in beneath it, preventing it from following the submersible head anymore and forming a seal against the aircraft's structure.

Mounted around the cable on the travelling head were four cable angle rollers. With the aircraft in the dipping hover with the submersible head underwater, any movement of the aircraft relative to the cable would be sensed by the cable touching the rollers. This sent a signal to the AFCS to adjust the aircraft's position and manoeuvre it back to a point where the

ABOVE View looking up through the belly of a Wessex HAS Mk.3 showing the Type 195 sonar transducer in the stowed position. *(Author)*

BELOW View of the sonar gear winch head showing the roller sensors which detected movement of the cable when in the 'dip'. *(Author)*

ASW sorties could often prove to be quite dull. In the days when there was a more relaxed attitude to flying, the devil made work for idle hands. In the 'dip' one warm night, one very bored Observer reportedly got out of his seat, slid open the cabin door, climbed up the side of the fuselage using the external footsteps and handholds and stood there for a few moments watching the right-hand pilot through the open door before nonchalantly tapping him on the shoulder. Luckily, the startled pilot's heart stayed beating!

Similarly, if there had been any friendly dispute between the front- and back-seat occupants – statement, followed by contradiction, then mild insult, personal abuse and sometimes even physical abuse – the Observer could quickly bring the pilot to heel by reaching up and giving a sharp tug on the exposed tail rotor cables that ran down the cabin roof above his head. The resulting unexpected and violent yaw was usually enough to quieten things down in the front. Reaching up under the seats and tying one of the pilots' bootlaces together and then waiting for him to try exiting the aircraft could also generate much entertainment for those in the back.

cable became recentralised again. In this way the aircraft would be kept in a steady position without the pilot having to make any inputs.

As the submersible head was winched back up, fins built into it would engage with angled fin guides in the circular, welded tube sonar well structure to ensure that it was aligned correctly. The trap doors would open and the head would engage again with the travelling head as it was raised up and into its stowed position in the cabin.

Doppler

Using an antenna contained within a square housing beneath the fuselage, the Doppler radar (Ryan APN-97A ARI.23075 for HAS Mk.1 and triple-beam microwave AW.96 ARI.5927 for HAS Mk.3) measured and indicated forward and

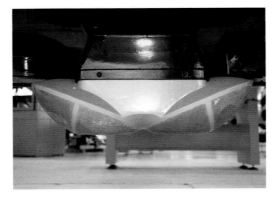

RIGHT Doppler aerial beneath the fuselage on a Wessex HAS Mk.1. *(Author)*

lateral velocity; ground speed and drift angle; measured vertical velocity and height; indicated aircraft position as a grid reference; and provided an output to the automatic stabilisation system for controlled hovering. When heading information was fed in, the system provided continuous automatic indication of aircraft position from a selected datum in nautical miles on four-digit in-line counters.

Radar

Perhaps the most distinguishing external feature of the Wessex HAS Mk.3 was the addition of the spine-mounted thimble radome assembly immediately aft of the main rotor gearbox fairings. This fairing protected the 24in-diameter Marconi lightweight radar scanner (ARI.5955), which had the lower 6in cut away, and which was designed to rotate through 360° in azimuth every second with a stabilised pencil beam of energy being sent out.

Aerodynamic tests during development showed that the radome caused directional stability problems through turbulence being created in the gap between the gearbox structure and the radome behind it which affected the tail rotor. To smooth out the airflow, an additional aerodynamic fairing was introduced which extended the aft end of the gearbox structure. The position, however, meant that radar coverage immediately ahead of the aircraft was not possible due to being blocked out by the main rotor pylon.

Electrical signals from the radar scanner were processed by a transmitter-receiver and amplifier control unit and projected via a CRT unit on to a large, circular PPI screen at the Observer's station on the port side of the cabin. This display was ground and north-stabilised and superimposed on to a plotting board.

The radar acted as a true motion navigation and action plot where two separate pictures could be maintained at different range scales and was used in conjunction with the sonar and the X-band secondary-radar transponder (ARI.5954) when two or more helicopters were co-operating in an attack on a sonar contact. An example would be the navigation plot to keep pace of where the parent ship was, and an action plot to fight the ASW action. Tracking contacts and carrying out navigation was achieved using acetate sheets laid over the PPI screen. The radar itself had a range against carrier-sized contacts of 35 nautical miles and frigate-sized contacts of 30 nautical miles.

Former Wessex HAS Mk.1 pilots found the advanced AFCS and Type 195M sonar in the HAS Mk.3 to be a major improvement, with demands for accurate flying between dips effectively disappearing. The Underwater Controller sat in the right-hand seat and worked the sonar in active and/or passive modes. The Observer, in the left-hand seat, was the tactician with the radar deciding where or what the submarine may do. Between the two of them, the back-seat crew would assess whether the sonar contact was indeed a submarine or something else!

If a submarine sonar contact had been made, rather than working out heading and times to the next dip position and then relying on the pilot to fly the transition profiles and headings, heights, and speeds accurately in order hopefully to make sonar contact again, all that was required was for the Observer to tell the pilot, 'Transition up and I'll tell you where to go.' The Observer would then use the radar to give directions to the pilot to fly the aircraft to the area of the next dip and give the instruction to 'mark dip here'.

The sonar range of the Type 195M was also much increased, meaning that an accurate new dip position was not as critical as it had been with the very limited sonar range of the Type 194 in the Wessex HAS Mk.1. Alternatively, the Observer could direct another helicopter to a position where it could also make sonar contact or drop a weapon if other aircraft were also available. Where the pilots could be of help in ASW work was in identifying surface contacts (especially in the radar blind arc forward caused by the main rotor pylon assembly) and trying to spot any periscopes!

Main rotor system

Main rotor head

The main rotor head (MRH), common to all Wessex variants, was fully articulated, mounted on and driven by the main rotor driveshaft from the main rotor gearbox (MRGB) and turned at 227rpm. The internally splined

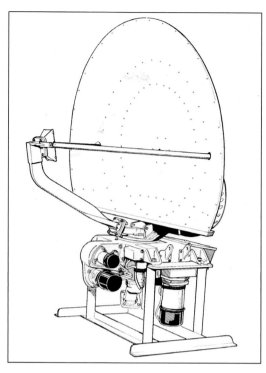

forged steel hub was held securely in place on two sets of split cones by a large heavily torque-loaded lock nut (known universally as the 'Jesus' nut due to the blasphemous utterance of maintenance personnel when trying to tighten or loosen it), which itself was located by a quadrant-shaped lock plate. The hub was capped at the upper and lower ends by top and bottom hub plates manufactured in a cruciform shape to provide four 'arm' mounting points. Between each of these points were attached a spacer (to carry loads between upper and lower plates), a blade damper (provided with hydraulic fluid from a reservoir on top of the head) and a trunnion.

The trunnion was also a forged steel assembly with the horizontal and vertical axes intersecting on the main rotor blade centreline and provided a hinge function, allowing for a limited amount of movement in the horizontal and vertical planes, known respectively as dragging and flapping. The horizontal pin through the trunnion and blade spindle constituted the flapping hinge while the dragging hinge was made possible by vertical spigots on the trunnion housing being mounted in bearings in the upper and lower hub plates, allowing it a degree of rotation.

Movement of the main rotor blades in the

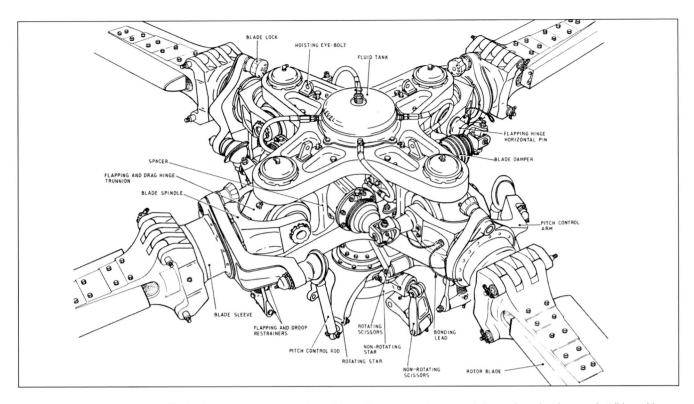

ABOVE Main rotor head. *(AP101C-0105)*

vertical plane was necessary to achieve the coning angle of the rotor disc to allow the aircraft to be controlled; however, this free movement posed a problem when the blades were stationary, or during start-up/shutdown when rotor rpm was low, or in gusty conditions when the blades were prone to a phenomenon called 'blade sail'.

With insufficient centrifugal force to keep the blades in a controllable range, and with nothing

to prevent them drooping low and striking either the aircraft or nearby personnel, a means of restraining this vertical movement was necessary. Attached to one end of each of the four trunnion arms were the sprung-loaded droop stop restrainer and flap assemblies. As the rotor rpm increased, so centrifugal force on the bob weights at the bottom of the restrainer would force its cam arm outwards and in doing so retract the droop restrainer flaps, allowing the blades

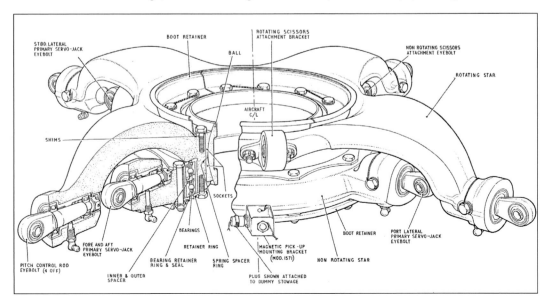

RIGHT Rotating and non-rotating star. *(AP101C-0101)*

greater vertical movement. As the rpm began to decay, the reverse would happen with the spring pressure now overcoming the rapidly reducing centrifugal force, allowing the cam arms to drop and thereby raise the droop restrainer stops to limit the blade movement. The bob weights were painted in a hi-viz paint to allow marshallers on the ground to see them and indicate to the pilot the transition period between the two where there was potential for blade sailing to occur.

Non-rotating star

Converting the linear movement of the stationary servo jacks to movements on the rotating MRH was achieved by using a rotating and non-rotating star assembly. A stationary non-rotating star with integral spherical bearing was slid over a splined guide around the main rotor gearbox output shaft. The star had four stub arms with eye bolts on each end. Three of these were connected to the output ends of the main rotor servos while the fourth was attached to one end of a non-rotating scissor link which connected to the main rotor gearbox casing.

Rotating star

Mounted to the inner race of the non-rotating star bearing via a ball and socket arrangement within its bore was the rotating star. Four large arms extended outwards, curving over the top of the non-rotating star such that the eyebolt bearings at each end were at the same level while a separate attachment bracket allowed another scissor link,

similar to that used on the non-rotating star, to connect the star boss with the underside of the main rotor hub bottom plate.

Main rotor pitch control rods

In the same way that control rods articulate the non-rotating star, so pitch change rods connected between the bearings on the rotating star and the MRH transmit movements from the rotating star to the MRH sleeves to alter the angles of the main rotor blades (MRBs).

Main rotor blades

The Wessex was fitted with four MRBs of all-metal construction, each measuring 26ft in span, 1.5ft chord and weighing 664lb. Twenty-three light alloy aerofoil-shaped skin sections were bonded to the rear edge of the single-piece, hollow-extruded aluminium leading edge spar and reinforced with internal channel-section ribs, each section being individually weighted for balance. Light alloy skins were then bonded to the top and bottom surfaces, their lipped forward edges being located in a groove machined into a rebate along the top of the spar. Neoprene rubber seals were fitted between each of the skin sections.

A 7° twist ran uniformly throughout the span to produce a washout towards the tip. Finally, balance weights were fitted at the end of the spar and enclosed by an aluminium tip fairing painted yellow to allow the rotor tips to be visible when rotating.

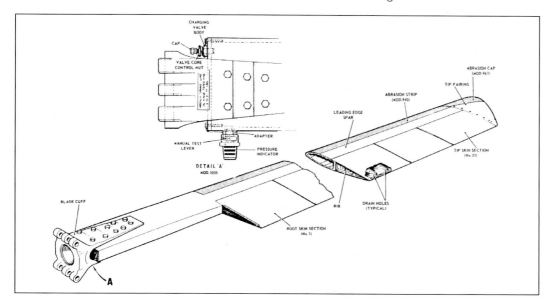

LEFT Main rotor blade construction, including BIM indicator.
(AP101C-0105)

RIGHT When folded,
the MRBs were held in
special blade pockets
attached to a saddle
frame secured to the
tailcone. *(Author)*

The blade spar root end slotted into a steel cuff, machined from a forging, which was then secured into position with 14 bolts. Each blade could then be fitted using two tapered steel pins inserted through a series of six knuckles which meshed with corresponding items on the MRH.

Damage to the spar, such as a crack, could be disastrous if not detected early. A simple, but effective, system known as Blade Inspection Method – BIM – was later introduced to give an early warning of any problems with the blades. The spar itself was sealed and filled with pressurised nitrogen gas via a charging point at the root end. This pressure operated a mechanical indicator located in a transparent capsule, also screwed into the root end, which consisted of two sliding cylinders – one black-striped and one white-striped. Under normal operation, the indicator showed solid white; however, if anything happened to compromise the spar or its components which allowed the gas to leak, the drop in pressure would cause the cylinders to move, progressively revealing the black stripes which would then become visible during servicing.

Transmission

The purpose of the Wessex's transmission system, as in all helicopters, was to translate the power from the engine into mechanical movement to drive the main and tail rotors, thereby generating lift and thrust. The transmission system comprised five main elements: the engine coupling gearbox, the main rotor gearbox (MRGB); a tail rotor driveshaft in six sections; an intermediate gearbox (IGB); and a tail rotor gearbox (TRGB).

Main rotor gearbox

Measuring some 4ft 9in × 5ft × 5ft 3in in height and, weighing in at 899lb, the MRGB was nearly as heavy as a concert grand piano.

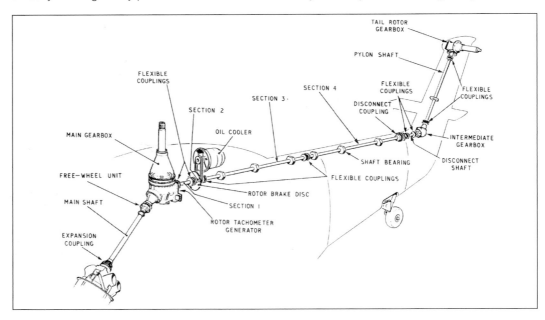

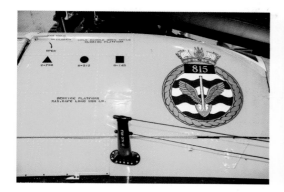

It consisted of five main sub-components: magnesium alloy input, upper and lower housings, the bearing support and the ring gear machined from high-tensile steel forgings.

A series of bracing and mounting struts, made from welded steel tubes with forged steel end fittings, attached at their upper ends to the MRGB upper housing and four similar welded tubular sway braces were bolted to the lower housing underneath. These tubes all came together to be welded at their outboard ends into fittings that formed 'feet', through which bolts secured the whole assembly to the transmission floor.

The upper housing supported the main rotor shaft, driven by ring and planet gears. The lower housing had mounting flanges for the input

FAR LEFT
Transmission access door on a Wessex HAS Mk.1. Royal Navy aircraft usually wore their parent unit's badge on these doors which, when opened, also acted as a servicing platform for maintenance personnel to stand on. *(Author)*

LEFT Transmission doors open on a Wessex HU Mk.5. *(Author)*

BELOW Schematic of the Wessex MRGB. *(AP101C-0105)*

BELOW Port side of the MRGB. The rotor brake can be seen far right. *(Author)*

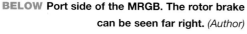

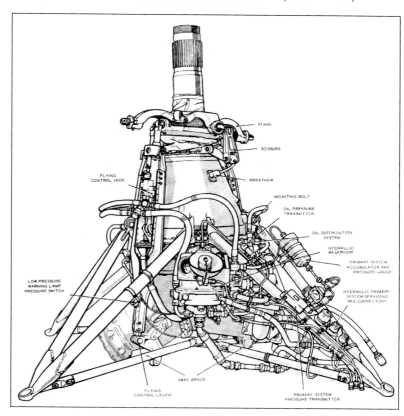

RIGHT Rotor brake master cylinder, pump handle and pressure gauge fitted to the starboard side of the cockpit overhead console. *(Author)*

BELOW Access panel in the starboard side of the tail pylon for access to the IGB (removed here). *(Author)*

shaft and auxiliary gearbox, as well as a sight glass for checking the oil levels.

Tail rotor driveshafts

There were effectively six tail rotor driveshafts, some made from hollow steel forgings and others from light aluminium, transmitting drive from the MRGB to the tail rotor and joined together by flexible couplings and bolts: Sections 1–4 of the intermediate shaft, a disconnect shaft and a pylon shaft.

Section 1 connected to the take-off flange at the rear of the MRGB to the Section 2 shaft. This was supported in ball bearings to a fitting on the transmission deck. The shaft also accommodated the main rotor brake disc and pulley which, via a belt, drove the oil cooler fan, forcing air through the oil radiator assembly.

Section 3 shaft fitted to the aft end of Section 2 and was joined to the forward end of Section 4 shaft, both of which continued along the inside of the upper part of the tailcone, supported in bearings bonded to the shafts themselves and held in place by bolts.

Rotor brake

A hydraulically operated rotor brake made up of a disc and three pairs of friction pads was installed at the Section 2 shaft to slow the rotor below 80rpm and to hold it stationary. A cylinder was fitted to the starboard outer face of the cockpit overhead console and the system pressurised by a large pump handle which pumped fluid from its own system that included a reservoir and accumulator to operate the friction pads.

Disconnect coupling

The disconnect coupling, as the name suggests, allowed the drive to the tail rotor to be disconnected quickly and easily without having to remove components, and in doing so allowed the tail pylon to be folded. This shortening of the aircraft's overall length enabled it to fit on aircraft carrier flight deck lifts and also made it easier to stow in the confines of a hangar.

The coupling was bolted to the hinge point of the tail pylon. A shaft, splined at both ends and held between bearings, had a toothed 'driven' coupling at its forward end and a 'driving' flange at its rear. Although the driven coupling was capable of sliding fore and aft along the splined shaft, a large spring behind it maintained sufficient forward force to ensure it was positively engaged with the coupling on the aft end of the Number 4 shaft.

When the tail pylon was unlocked, opened

and folded, the spring forced the driven coupling to its furthest forward position where its teeth engaged with a simple locking plate. The plate prevented the coupling from moving and thus stopped the tail rotor from turning. When the tail pylon was closed and locked again, the driven coupling meshed with the Number 4 shaft and was pushed aft against the spring, disengaging the locking plate and allowing the tail rotor to move once again with the rest of the tail rotor drive system.

Intermediate gearbox

The IGB was mounted within the tail pylon and changed the angle of the tail rotor drive to the pylon driveshaft which ran through the inside of the tail pylon to the tail rotor gearbox. It was comprised of three separate cast light alloy flanged housings: input, centre and output – which were secured together with bolts and nuts.

Tail rotor gearbox

The TRGB changed the direction of drive from the intermediate gearbox through 90° and reduced the rotational speed by approximately half. For the Gazelle-powered variants this was 1,318rpm. The TRGB also provided a means of varying the pitch of the tail rotor by housing the pitch-change mechanism.

Tail rotor hub

The tail rotor hub was internally splined to allow it to fit on to the output shaft of the TRGB. On

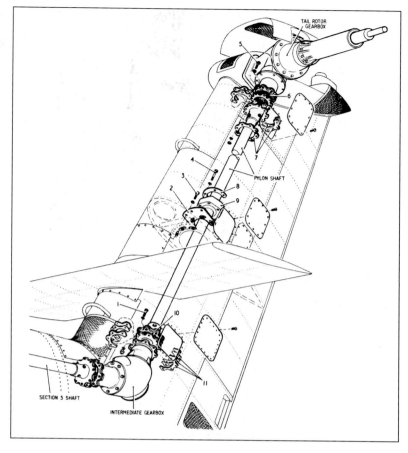

each of the four stub arms were mounted blade spindles, their forked ends being held in place by bolts and allowed to rotate about two sets of needle roller bearings. Fitted to the outer end of the spindles, and allowed to rotate via a stack of five roller bearings, were cylindrical blade

ABOVE Detail of the tail pylon showing the installation of the pylon shaft and both IGB and TRGB. *(AP101C-0105)*

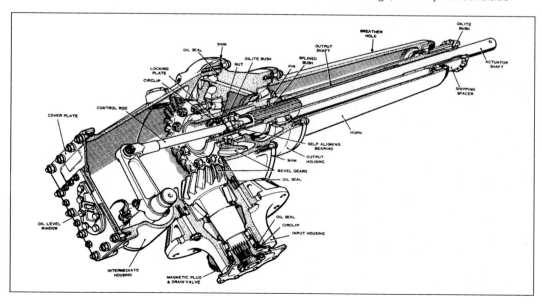

LEFT Cutaway of the TRGB showing the integral pitch change mechanism. *(AP101C-0105)*

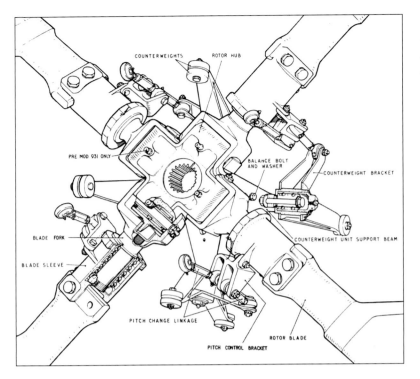

ABOVE **Tail rotor hub
and blade assembly.**
(Author)

RIGHT **TRGB with
tail rotor hub still
attached.** *(Author)*

BELOW **Tail rotor
servo on the port side
of the transmission
deck.** *(Author)*

sleeves. The outboard ends of these sleeves
were fork-shaped, allowing each tail rotor blade
to slot into position and be held in position by
two bolts.

Pitch-change mechanism

A four-armed pitch-change beam was fitted to
the end of the TRGB pitch control shaft. Each
arm end was forked to allow the fitting of a
pitch change link. These links consisted of two
spherical bearing ends screwed into a rod. The
length of the links could be altered by turning
the rod with a spanner to effectively screw the
ends in and out.

The other end of the pitch-change
link was connected to the inner fork of
a double-forked bracket attached to the
outer casing of the blade sleeve. Movement
of the pitch-change beam, which runs
through the hollow centre of the output drive
shaft, caused the links to move inboard
or outboard. As they did so, they pulled/
pushed on the off-centre fork on the blade
sleeve, causing it to rotate and thereby
altering the pitch of the blades.

All four blades were affected equally to
increase or decrease tail rotor thrust to counter
the torque reaction of the main rotor and
thereby provide directional control.

Tail rotor balancing

Fitted in between the tail rotor hub and the
TRGB was a counterweight unit consisting of
a series of four cranked support beams and

BELOW **Wessex HU Mk.5 tail rotor.** *(Author)*

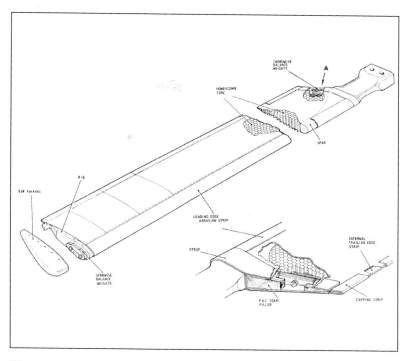

brackets and corresponding weights which automatically reduced control loads. These beams were connected to the outer fork of the double fork bracket on the blade sleeves.

Tail rotor blades

Four tail rotor blades were attached, each via two nuts, bolts and balancing spacers at the root end, to the forked ends of the tail rotor blade sleeves. Each blade comprised a light alloy spar which formed the leading edge and the flat root end through which the mounting bolts passed. Weights were attached at the outer end of the spar to give span-wise balancing.

Attached to the rear of the spar was a honeycomb core around which was a light alloy skin, itself bonded to the spar at the forward end and sealed with a capping strip to form the trailing edge. A stainless steel tip fairing was riveted to the end of the blade and a stainless steel abrasion strip protected the leading edge of the spar.

With the exception of the erosion strip and tip fairing, each blade was painted. The inboard section was Medium Sea Grey while the outer section was alternate red, white and red to allow the tail rotor disc to be visible while turning. This later changed to green with red tips on some aircraft.

Transmission oil system

The main, intermediate and tail rotor gearboxes and expansion coupling all had their own independent oil supplies, filled via plugs in their casings with the fluid levels visible through sight glasses. The freewheel unit had its own reservoir installed immediately in front of the MRGB.

ABOVE Tail rotor blade construction. *(AP101-0105)*

BELOW Oil cooler aft of the MRGB with tail rotor servo beneath. The pipes from the rear of the cooler fed air to the fuel tanks to provide pressurisation. *(Author)*

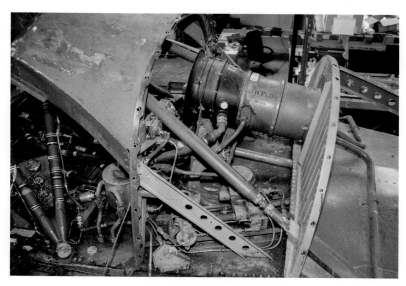

RIGHT Right-hand pilot's cyclic stick grip.
(Author)

RIGHT Left-hand pilot's collective lever.
(Author)

BELOW Right-hand pilot's collective lever and friction lock.
(Author)

Flying controls

For a helicopter to achieve controlled flight it requires three basic primary flying controls: cyclic, collective and yaw.

Cyclic control

As the rotor blades rotate they prescribe a horizontal disc with lift being generated at 90° to it. By altering the angle of this disc, the movement and direction of the helicopter can be controlled: forward, back, left and right. This is achieved by altering the pitch of each blade in a cyclic variation: increasing lift in one sector and simultaneously decreasing lift in the directly opposing sector. In doing so this causes the rotor blades on one side of the disc to flap up and the corresponding opposite blades to flap down, thus effectively tilting the disc. This results in the direction of lift changing, causing the helicopter to alter direction in response.

In order to make these changes, cyclic sticks were positioned in front of the cockpit seats between the pilot's knees. Movement of the cyclic stick allowed inputs to control the fore, aft and lateral movement of the helicopter by altering the pitch of the main rotor blades individually. The handgrips at the top of the sticks were fitted with switches and buttons to operate various systems including the AFCS cut-out, cyclic trim and press-to-transmit radio button.

Collective control

While use of the cyclic stick to tilt the rotor disc would produce a change in direction of the lift force to effect directional changes, in order to generate and control lift all four of the Wessex MRBs needed to be increased or decreased simultaneously and by the same amount. This is called collective control.

To achieve this, a collective lever was situated to the left-hand side of both cockpit seats. As with the cyclic stick, the hand grip on the top of the pilot's collective lever contained switches and buttons for underslung load jettison, landing light control, flotation system, rescue hoist control and collective AFCS channel release to be operated conveniently. Although the positioning of these buttons reduced the need for the pilot to take his hands off the controls, should he have needed to, then a locking device was fitted to the first pilot's stick only, consisting of a split collar around the lever which could be tightened by a handle to control the amount of friction applied to allow the lever's position to be maintained hands-free.

In the event of an emergency, such as engine failure, the aircraft could enter what is known as 'autorotation'. By lowering the collective lever fully to reduce pitch on the MRBs, the aircraft would begin to descend rapidly. As it did so, air would flow up through the main rotor disc causing the blades to continue rotating. At a predetermined height, the pilot would flare the aircraft by pulling back on the cyclic stick to raise the nose and reduce forward speed.

Doing so, however, would actually cause the main rotor speed (known as Nr) to begin to rise. To contain this increase and thereby prevent damage that would otherwise be caused by the main rotor overspeeding, the pilot would have to carefully use small amounts of collective lever inputs. As the MRBs met the air at this increased angle of attack, so they would generate increased drag, helping to counter this speed increase and bringing it back into limits.

But too much collective input would induce a greater amount of drag than was necessary to control the Nr, causing a rapid decay in the kinetic energy stored up in the rotor system and slowing the blades to a point where they would no longer generate any lift, whereupon the helicopter would simply fall out of the sky.

Maintaining this fine balancing act between Nr, lift and gravity would enable the rate of descent to be controlled until the helicopter was within approximately 10ft of the ground, whereupon the pilot could progressively raise the collective lever all the way up, sacrificing all of the remaining Nr energy to generate a final amount of lift sufficient to help cushion the landing.

Collective interlinks

Operation of the collective lever can, however, produce unwanted aerodynamic side effects. For example, raising the collective causes the nose of the aircraft to naturally rise which will lead to a reduction in air speed. To minimise these effects, mechanical 'interlinks' consisting of a spring box with a set of levers and cranks are fitted beneath the cockpit floor. These combine the collective inputs with other controls to change the effect on the aircraft.

The collective-to-fore/aft interlink beneath the cockpit floor automatically applies an amount of nose-down cyclic movement to compensate for this nose-up movement. Conversely, lowering the collective causes the nose to drop which is countered by the interlink automatically generating a backwards cyclic input to bring the nose back up again.

Likewise, altering the collective input changes the main rotor torque effect, causing the aircraft to yaw. Increasing the input makes the nose yaw to the right while decreasing causes it to yaw to the left.

Main rotor servos

Although early helicopters were simple and light enough to be flown with manual flying controls, the effort needed to overcome the aerodynamic forces on the main and tail rotor blades to effect any manoeuvring nonetheless made it at best a tiring experience.

To relieve the pilot of this strenuous task all but the most basic of helicopters these days have hydraulically assisted powered flying controls. Unlike most newer and larger helicopters, the Wessex had the ability to revert to manual control should the hydraulic systems fail.

Cyclic pitch (fore and aft cyclic stick movement) and collective pitch inputs from the pilot's controls were transmitted via push-pull rods, bellcranks and quadrants to the secondary servo unit and mixing unit where they were combined. From here, mechanical linkages fed the outputs to the primary servo jacks. These jacks operated independently of each other to tilt the non-rotating star assembly in the fore/aft and lateral planes to achieve cyclic pitch (nose up or down) and lateral (banking left or right) control, and in unison to govern collective pitch (climb or descend).

Yaw control

Sir Isaac Newton's Third Law of Motion, which states that for every action there is an equal and opposite reaction, means that with the main rotor spinning in one direction and generating torque, the fuselage suspended beneath will naturally try to rotate in the opposite direction and cause loss of directional control. To counteract and control

this reactionary force, a vertically mounted, four-bladed tail rotor was fitted.

In the cockpit, a set of rudder pedals were mounted on cross tubes in the footwells of both first and second pilot positions. Each pair were adjustable in their positioning via a small handwheel mounted between each set to allow for pilots with longer or shorter legs to reach them comfortably.

Inputs from the pedals were fed via levers and push-pull rods to a quadrant mounted on the aircraft's centreline at the forward end of the cockpit interseat console immediately behind the forward sloping bulkhead. At this quadrant, the control was converted from rods to braided metal cables which ran back outboard along the front of the cockpit, using pulleys mounted in brackets to alter the direction of the cable routing, guided through fairleads in the frames along the inside of the cockpit structure and cabin sides to a pedestal unit and tail rotor servo on the port side of the transmission decking.

Both cables wrapped around a set of pulleys mounted on either end of a pivoted arm assembly. While the port cable was then allowed to pass uninterrupted straight through the middle of the body of the servo in guides to the aft quadrant, the starboard cable passed through the hollow piston rod of the servo unit and was held in place by a spherical stop on the end. As the cables moved, so the pulley arm pivoted. This movement caused a hydraulic pilot valve on the servo jack to operate, directing hydraulic fluid into one side of the servo jack and, depending on which side of the jack the fluid is directed into, forcing it to move one way or another. In doing so, the cable attached

to the outside moved. As the body of the servo jack moved in one direction, so the pulley arm automatically became repositioned, recentring the pilot valve, shutting off the flow of hydraulic fluid and therefore stopping any more movement until further input was sensed.

The two cables continued on from here, swapping over sides, supported by pulleys running along the sides of the tailcone internal structure. The starboard cable featured a spring cylinder: a cylindrical barrel housing attached to one end of the cable with the other attached to a piston rod held in a retracted position within the barrel by double springs which helped to damp out vibrations fed back from the tail rotor blades to the servo unit.

The cables were now secured to the aft ends of a two-part quadrant, mounted on the aft-most frame bulkhead of the tailcone. The mounting bolt allowed the two halves to rotate as one unit but also allowed each half to pivot independently, their position relative to each other being governed by a spring unit fitted between the open forward ends of the quadrant. This spring kept the two ends of the quadrant apart and acted as a cable tension regulator by expanding (and thus tautening the cable) or contracting (thus slackening the cable) depending upon ambient temperature to ensure that the cable remained at the right tension in all conditions.

Control movement was then transmitted up through the tail pylon via levers, cranks and push-pull rods to the TRGB.

Flight control system

The flight control system on the Wessex comprised four sub-systems: an autostabiliser, an autopilot, a flight director and an ASW system. These relied upon inputs from vertical references, navigation, compass, air speed, barometric and radio altimeters, the sonar and the Doppler equipment. The outputs from the system were used to control the aircraft in pitch, yaw and altitude channels of the flying control using a series of actuators.

Autostabiliser

The autostabiliser was a duplicate system controlling the aircraft in pitch, roll and a limited amount in the yaw channels.

Autopilot

The Autopilot Mk.19 was used in conjunction with the autostabiliser to include heading, air speed and height hold and to control automatic turns using the pitch, roll, collective and yaw channels. The system was fed with data from a series of gyros, barometric sensors positioned around the aircraft, and from control position transmitters operated by the cyclic and collective levers in the cockpit.

Any deviation from the aircraft's set attitude in pitch and roll would be sensed by vertical gyros. The 'error' would be computed and electrical signals sent to servo motors within the flying control system linkages to automatically make adjustments in order to return the aircraft to the correct attitude.

Altitude control was governed by changes in barometric pressure, while yaw (directional) control was effected by reference to the aircraft's compass. A control unit for the system was fitted on the interseat console in the cockpit.

Flight director

The flight director monitored the performance of the autopilot, controlling the pitch, roll, yaw and altitude of the aircraft.

ASW system

The ASW system was used in conjunction with the autopilot to provide control of the specialist services associated with the role: controlling the descent of the aircraft to a hover height (known as 'Transition Down'); to maintain a steady hover position while the sonar body was submerged beneath the surface of the water (known as the 'dip') to prevent any relative movement between the body and the water and to keep the body positioned upright; and to programme the climb out from the dip to a preset height (known as 'Transition Up').

Hydraulic system

Aerodynamic and physical forces acting on the flying controls of helicopters can be extremely high, making control of the aircraft difficult, tiring and often impossible. To help to overcome these forces and achieve almost effortless control, the main and tail rotors of large helicopters are normally controlled by hydraulic actuators that amplify small input movements into large output forces.

The Wessex had three main independent hydraulic systems, all operating independently of each other: primary, secondary and hoist. Both the primary and secondary hydraulic systems functioned when the engines were running and the rotor turning. For the ASW variants there was also an additional system which operated the sonar winching equipment.

Primary system

The main purpose of the primary system was to power the primary servo jacks which acted upon the non-rotating star controlling the main rotor and absorbing the flight control loads. Hydraulic fluid stored in a reservoir within the fairing aft of the MRGB was pumped through a micronic pressure filter and via rigid metal pipes to the three servo jacks mounted on the gearbox itself.

Primary servo jacks

One end of each of the three primary servo jacks was mounted on the MRGB, and at the opposite end to the non-rotating star. The flying control system was connected to the pilot control valve assembly on the body of the jack. Small movements brought about by the movement of the flying controls would open and close this valve which in turn allowed pressurised hydraulic fluid to enter the main body to force the piston inside to move in or out. Movement of this piston would cause the control valve to recentralise, shutting off the flow of more fluid, thus stopping the jack from moving any further.

Secondary system

The secondary servo jacks formed part of the flying control linkage to the main rotor to transmit control movements as a hydro-mechanical linkage but did not take on any load-sharing. The secondary hydraulic system also operated the flying controls when the flight control system was engaged. In the event of a primary system failure, the secondary system would allow the pilot to control the aircraft enough to make an emergency landing.

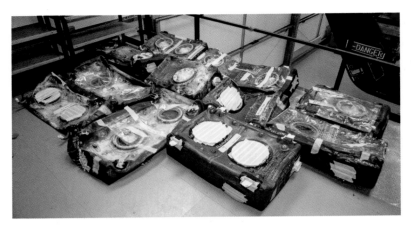

ABOVE Eleven of the thirteen bag tanks removed from a Wessex HU Mk.5. *(Author)*

BELOW Layout of the Wessex fuel tanks and tank groups. *(AP101C-0105)*

BOTTOM Pipes from the oil cooler provide air pressure to the fuel tanks. *(Author)*

Fuel system

Although all Wessex shared the same basic fuselage, the type of engine and role configuration had a significant effect on how many fuel tanks it was fitted with. The HAS Mk.1, for instance, had 11, the HAS Mk.3 9, and the HU Mk.5 13. In all cases, however, they were interconnected, flexible, crash-proof fuel tanks built into the fuselage and arranged in two distinct groups: a forward group and an aft group.

Tank groups

The forward group on all variants comprised three sets of tanks – Numbers 1, 2 and 3. The aft tank group was where the differences were to be found: two further sets of tanks for the HAS Mk.1 (Numbers 4 and 5), one for the HAS Mk.3 (Number 4), three for the HU Mk.5 and Mk.60 (Numbers 4, 5 and 6).

For the Gnome-powered variants, the forward group supplied the starboard engine while the aft group supplied the port engine.

Numbers 1 and 6 tanks were single units, both of which were positioned higher than the others above the cabin floor level: Number 1 in a fireproof casing forward of the front bulkhead as part of the forward group and Number 6 aft of the rear bulkhead on the starboard side as part of the aft group. Each was fitted with its own gravity filler point.

Numbers 2, 3, 4 and 5, meanwhile, were situated under the cabin floor and were, themselves, subdivided into port and starboard sets of individual tanks.

Tanks 2 and 4, however, featured one more tank: a centre tank. These centre tanks were fitted with sumps containing submerged, electrically driven booster pumps, and acted as collector tanks for their respective groups, progressively taking fuel from the others.

In the Gazelle-powered variants, the fuel from the Number 4 centre tank was transferred forward to the Number 2 centre tank and thence to the engine; in the Gnome-powered aircraft, the two were separate, with the Number 2 centre tank from the forward group feeding the starboard engine and the Number 4 centre tank from the aft group supplying the port engine.

With rotors disengaged, all of the tanks were vented to atmosphere. However, once the rotors were engaged, pipes from the transmission oil cooler fan provided slight pressurisation into the Number 3, 4 and 5 sets of tanks to aid fuel flow.

From the booster pumps, fuel flowed through the respective mechanical LP cocks to the motorised cross-feed cock. This was normally closed, but if one pump failed, it could be opened to allow fuel to be supplied to both engines from one pump. From here, the fuel passed through non-return valves and a fuel flow transmitter to the centrifugal filter on the respective engine.

STARBOARD ENGINE SUPPLY   PORT ENGINE SUPPLY

| 1 | 2 | 3 | 4 | 5 | 6 |

FUEL TANK ARRANGEMENT

| Variant | Tank group number | | | | | | Total |
| | Forward group | | | Aft group | | | |
	1	2	3	4	5	6	
HAS Mk.1	*	*	*	*	*		11
HC Mk.2	*	*	*	*	*	*	13
HAS Mk.3	*	*	*	*			9
HCC Mk.4	*	*	*	*	*	*	13
HU Mk.5	*	*	*	*	*	*	13
HAS Mk.31	*	*	*	*			9
Mk.60	*	*	*	*	*	*	13

Gravity refuelling

To gravity refuel the forward group, fuel entered via the Number 1 tank filler point and flowed through non-return valves into the Number 2 and 3 sets of tanks until they were all full, whereupon the Number 1 tank topped up. Similarly, for the aft group, fuel entered via the Number 6 tank filler, through valves and into Numbers 5 and 4 tanks before finally filling Number 6.

Pressure refuelling, defuelling and jettisoning

Separate pressure refuel/defuel couplings were situated on the starboard side of the aircraft. These were generally beneath the cabin floor level, with the exception of the HAS Mk.3 whose forward point was housed within an aerodynamic-shaped fairing immediately forward of the cabin door. Unlike the gravity points, these couplings were connected to Number 1 and Number 4 tanks (Number 6 tank on the HU Mk.5), allowing both forward and aft groups to be filled simultaneously from either one. When the tanks were full, internal float switches operated to energise the refuel/defuel valve, preventing any further transfer of fuel.

In order to suction defuel the aircraft for maintenance, both Numbers 2 and 4 centre tanks had special valves fitted within the sumps. Similarly, in an emergency, electrically operated jettison valves could be opened via a switch on the main instrument panel in the cockpit, allowing fuel to be pumped through pipes protruding through the aircraft's belly into jettison pipes and hoses fitted on the underside and out to the atmosphere. The hoses

LEFT Aft gravity refuelling point with earthing point and guarded selector switches on the side of a Wessex HU Mk.5. *(Author)*

LEFT Pressure refuelling point within an aerodynamic fairing forward of the cabin door on a Wessex HAS Mk.3. *(Author)*

LEFT The aft pressure refuel/defuel valve and fuel jettison pipe with hinged link beneath a Wessex HU Mk.5. *(Author)*

themselves were mounted on an articulated strut which allowed them to be deflected out of the way in the event of the aircraft landing on uneven ground and then dropped back to their original position again when airborne.

Helicopter in-flight refuelling

In some instances, such as if an undercarriage oleo became damaged or a flight deck was obstructed, an aircraft may not have been able to land to take on more fuel when it needed to. In this instance, helicopter in-flight refuelling – HIFR – was used.

A special refuelling hose would be winched up from the ground or flight deck using the aircraft's winch while it maintained a steady, low hover. The aircrewman in the cabin doorway would then attach the hose to the refuelling coupling on the side of the aircraft and the

refuelling would begin. In an emergency, or if the load on the hose exceeded a certain figure, weak links in the hose would break, allowing the aircraft to fly away with the remaining parts suspended beneath the winch.

Long-range tanks

On the Royal Navy and Royal Australian Navy variants, two externally mounted, aerodynamically shaped drop tanks could be fitted on the weapon carriers – one either side – with a capacity of either 97 or 100 gallons each, extending the range of the aircraft.

Pressurised by air bled from the engine compressors via the cabin heating ducting, the starboard drop tank fed into the Number 1 tank while the one on the port side fed into the Number 6 tank via the pressure refuelling coupling.

Auxiliary tanks

For the HC Mk.2, a different type of long-range fuel system was devised. This consisted of two 110-gallon cylindrical fuel tanks mounted side by side in the cabin which would begin emptying once 40 gallons had been used from the aircraft's own two groups of main tanks.

Undercarriage

All Wessex variants featured the same non-retractable undercarriage arrangement: two large fixed mainwheels at the front and one smaller castoring wheel at the rear.

BELOW Wessex HU
Mk.5 XT766 ('512/
PO') of 772 NAS fitted
with the external long-
range fuel tank on the
port weapons carrier.
(Author's collection)

Main undercarriage

The main undercarriage consisted of a large oleo-pneumatic shock absorber strut attached to the fuselage below the cockpit via a universal joint and a steel tube radius strut which was bent at its inboard end to fit into aluminium bronze support bearings in the lower fuselage.

The shock absorber strut was made up of a fixed cylinder and a piston tube. Within the piston tube was a mixture of hydraulic fluid and compressed air in direct contact with each other. As weight was put on to the oleo, so the cylinder would travel up the piston tube, forcing the hydraulic fluid within the cylinder into the piston through an internal restriction orifice. This further compressed the air within the piston and damped the recoil action of the oleo, lessening the likelihood of the aircraft bouncing back into the air.

The two struts joined at a forged fitting on to which the forged steel axle assembly was installed. A flange for the wheel brake unit and attachment points for the fitting of the flotation equipment cool gas generator were also built into the axle assembly, as well as a lug for towing the aircraft on the ground.

The large, balloon-type tyres, inflated to a pressure of 45psi, gave the aircraft good soft-ground operational capabilities, preventing it from sinking into the surface.

Wheel brakes

Hydraulically operated brakes were fitted to both mainwheels, controlled by the movement of piston rods of master cylinders fitted to the sides of the pilot's rudder pedals and activated by hinged toe plates. Independent operation of the brakes gave differential braking during taxiing of the aircraft. By depressing both toe plates at the same time and selecting a lever on the interseat console in the cockpit to the 'PARKED' position, the brakes could be locked on. To disengage the parking brake, the toe pedals had to be depressed again before selecting the lever to 'OFF'.

Tailwheel

The tailwheel, the tyre of which was also pumped up to 45psi – an easy figure to remember when 'out in the field' – attached to a steel axle on a single, forged aluminium fork assembly which was mounted into a cylindrical housing at the aft end of a magnesium alloy

ABOVE LEFT
Starboard main undercarriage. *(Author)*

ABOVE **Starboard main undercarriage radius strut with built-in footsteps.** *(Author)*

BELOW **Tailwheel assembly. The tailwheel lock actuating cable can just be seen running through the middle of the casting.** *(Author)*

Maintaining balance in any rotating object is crucial to ensuring that the forces acting upon it are contained. Failure to do so can cause these forces to become destructive in a very short period of time. Helicopters, of course, are no exception.

Those fitted with an articulated MRH, such as the Wessex, are susceptible to a dangerous phenomenon known as 'ground resonance' where out-of-balance oscillations can literally tear the aircraft apart if prompt actions are not taken.

Under normal operation, the MRH drag hinge dampers allow each of the rotor blades to lead (advance forward) or lag (retreat backwards) in the horizontal plane to ensure that they assume and then maintain an equal spacing between each other, thus preserving the centre of gravity about the rotor mast and thereby keeping the whole rotor assembly in balance.

On rotor engagement, the aircraft can briefly be seen – and felt – to rock from side to side, back and forth as the dampers allow the blades to assume their natural position, but this quickly dissipates. If, however, the dampers are either incorrectly maintained or are unserviceable, then the blades cannot assume their correct positioning and the centre of gravity shifts further away from the rotor head. As the rotor increases in speed, so the oscillations worsen, rapidly reaching a dangerous level.

While on the ground, dampening of these oscillations is reliant upon the absorption by the undercarriage. If, however, either of the oleo legs or tyres are of differential pressures then this can exacerbate the problem.

At low rpm, the pilot can elect to shut the aircraft down; however, if ground resonance occurs at high rpm then prompt action has to be taken. Left unchecked, the oscillations will increase to a level where the rocking motion causes the aircraft to topple over on to its side. Although counter-intuitive, by promptly raising the collective and lifting the aircraft into a low hover, the airframe is free to move independently of the ground, allowing it to effectively dampen the oscillations and the rotor blades are given a chance to reposition themselves before a landing is attempted and the aircraft safely shut down. This is a last-ditch course of action, and rotor damper, oleo and tyre pressure checks are of prime importance.

BELOW What happens when a Wessex undercarriage is not properly maintained. Wessex XR509 ('AK') of 72 Squadron lies on its side after encountering ground resonance at RAF Odiham, 6 October 1981. *(Author's collection)*

yoke casting. This yoke was attached at its forward end to the tailcone by a bolted hinge arrangement and at the aft end was supported by an oleo-pneumatic shock absorber.

The fork assembly was allowed to rotate within the yoke and thereby let the aircraft manoeuvre on the ground. To return the tailwheel to the fore and aft position in flight, a cam at the upper end of a strong coiled spring in the cylindrical housing came into contact with a fixed cam at the top of the shaft which forced the fork back into alignment.

When not manoeuvring, the tailwheel was normally locked in the fore and aft position by operating a control handle at the bottom of the pilot's instrument panel. This connected to a series of cables that ran down the starboard side of the cabin roof, guided by pulleys and a spring box assembly, along the lower edge of the tailcone internal structure to move a locking pin in the base of the yoke casting next to the fork assembly. When locked, the pin engaged through a collar, locking the fork to the yoke and preventing it from rotating. A metal indicator plate at the top of the yoke served to provide a visual indication that the tailwheel was locked.

Electrical system

All Wessex variants had two types of electrical system: direct current (DC) and alternating current (AC). These could be generated externally on the ground or internally when the aircraft was rotors-running. Both systems had their own series of busbars through which power was distributed to the various systems.

Batteries

Within the avionics bay in the starboard side of the nose was a 24V 15-ampere hour lead-acid battery (two of them coupled in parallel on the HU Mk.5 with the HCC Mk.4 having two 18-ampere hour versions), sufficient enough for a limited number of internal starts without ground power, and a 24V 7-ampere hour emergency alkaline battery used for hoist cable-cutter operation, standby cockpit lighting and for powering critical instruments such as the standby artificial horizon and

standby compass and operation of the standby UHF radio in the event of electrical system failure.

External ground power

For operation of the electrical system on the ground without using the battery or during servicing, a socket was built into the starboard side of the nose, protected by a quick-release hinged flap, for the connection of a 28V DC ground supply. This was selected using the 'GROUND-FLIGHT' battery master switch in the cockpit.

Internal power

On the Gazelle-powered Wessex HAS Mk.1 and Mk.3, with the engine running and rotors engaged, two generators provided a 28V DC supply: one mounted on the engine and the other on the rear of the MRGB.

Three inverters provided AC electrical power to the aircraft. Numbers 1 and 2 inverters served three AC distribution busbars: cruise (for the pilot's attitude indicator, identification friend or foe (IFF)), hover (for the Doppler radar and radio altimeter) and essential (all other systems critical for the safe operation of the aircraft). Number 3 alternator served the ground instruments busbar, powering the fuel contents indicator, engine oil pressure, jet pipe temperature and fuel flow meter gauges for start-up and in the event of an emergency.

On the HAS Mk.1, two 10kVA alternators – one mounted at the front of the engine and one on the port side of the MRGB – supplied with a 200V AC system. On the Wessex HAS Mk.3, a third alternator, known as the pulse load generator, was also driven by the MRGB which produced 27V DC to power the four sonar transmitters.

Part of the aircraft's AC output was also fed through two transformer rectifier units (TRU) mounted in the avionics bay on the port side of the nose. These TRUs converted the AC power into a 28V DC output. For the Gnome-powered variants, two engine-driven 6kW generators were fitted to the coupling gearbox. Two inverters ('NORMAL' and 'STANDBY') were fitted in the port nose avionics compartment to provide 200V AC and 115V AC supplies.

RIGHT White identification light on the underside of the tailcone. *(Author)*

RIGHT Nite Sun infra-red searchlight fitted to the starboard undercarriage of a 28 (AC) Squadron Wessex HC Mk.2.
(Pete Wendes)

ABOVE Light on the port main undercarriage. *(Author)*

RIGHT Forward strobe lights within protective Perspex bubble on the starboard side of the nose of Wessex HCC Mk.4 XV733. *(Author)*

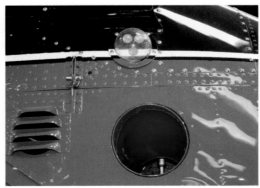

External lighting

As with all aircraft, the Wessex was fitted with a series of external lights and lamps to both assist with carrying out the various roles and also to increase the aircraft's visibility.

Navigation lighting

Coloured navigational lights were fitted either side of the nose: green for starboard and red for port. A white light was fitted at the aft end of a fairing on the tail pylon. These lights could all be selected to bright or dim and to steady or flashing for increased conspicuity or for signalling reasons.

Identification lamps

A downward identification lamp was fitted on the lower structure of the aircraft at the forward end of the tailcone.

Landing, search and flood lamps

A 450W, steerable and retractable search lamp was fitted in a housing on the underside of the nose, controlled by two electrical motors. On the HCC Mk.4, this lamp was repositioned on the nose door. On the HU Mk.5C aircraft converted for RAF use, three additional flood lamps were introduced – one on each main undercarriage radius arm and one on a bracket attached to the tailcone – to help with night search and rescue operations. An additional flood lamp was fitted to the hoist support assembly rear strut on a steerable mount that could be manually operated by the aircrewman to point in any direction so desired.

Hoist and emplaning lamp

To aid with trooping operations and use of the hoist, a single white emplaning light was fitted within a small fairing above the cabin door.

Anti-collision lamps

On the HC Mk.2, HCC Mk.4 and HU Mk.5, a motorised Grimes anti-collision beacon was mounted atop the same fairing as the tail navigational light. The HCC Mk.4 had an additional, identical beacon on the nose door. Two partially mirrored bulbs were installed diagonally opposite each other on a geared plate which rotated within a red-tinted glass cover to give a flashing red light effect.

Later, on the HC Mk.2, the anti-collision beacon was replaced by a dual-colour high-intensity strobe light, installed in the same position and consisting of two xenon flash tubes capable of emitting intensified bursts of either white, for normal daytime operations, or red light for use with night vision goggles (NVG) installed within a triangular-shaped glass lens.

The Wessex HCC Mk.4 featured a set of white anti-collision strobe lights fitted beneath Perspex covers on either side of the nose, together with one on the tail as per the HC Mk.2.

Communications system

The Wessex had two radio compartments: one in the port side of the nose above the engine bay where the majority of the equipment was contained, the size and shape of which differing with engine installation, and the other being in the rear fuselage aft of the main cabin.

HF radio

All marks of Wessex were fitted with a Collins 618-T (ARI.23090) HF transceiver/receiver unit for long-range voice communication. The aerial for the system consisted of a series of fixed wires rigged between six insulated masts running down and along the outside of the rear fuselage.

UHF radio

UHF communications were achieved using the lightweight, 12 preset channel PTR 170 (ARI.18197 for the HAS Mk.3 and HU Mk.5C) or 19 preset channel AN/ARC.52 (ARI.18124 for the HAS Mk.1 and HU Mk.5) UHF and homing radios. Two dipole blade homing aerials were mounted beneath the nose of the aircraft for homing and communications with another fitted on the upper fuselage aft of the radome purely for communications. The frequency range of the radio allowed the homing facility for search and rescue operations to function on the international distress frequency, known as 'Guard'.

The standby UHF radio (ARI.23057 for the HAS Mk.1, HC Mk.2 and HU Mk.5 or ARI.23159 for the HAS Mk.3 and HU Mk.5C) was fitted in the aft radio compartment for use when the aircraft's DC electrical system or main UHF radio failed and also operated on 'Guard'. The associated whip aerial was mounted beneath the tailcone.

Transponder

To allow the aircraft to be identified as 'friendly' by a ground radar station, the PTR 446 IFF (ARI.5970/1 and ARI.5970/3 for HAS Mk.3) airborne radar equipment formed part of the IFF/Secondary Surveillance Radar system.

When 'interrogated' by radar, the system transmitted a coded response back to identify itself. If correct, it would be seen to be a 'friend'; if incorrect it would be deemed to be a 'foe'. The transponder unit for the system was fitted in a mounting tray on the starboard side of the floor.

Armament

Being very much a product of the Cold War, the Wessex in all of its military guises was capable of carrying an impressive array of external armament ranging from guns, anti-submarine depth charges, flares and even an atomic depth charge.

External stores carriers

Two electrically operated weapon carriers were introduced which allowed the Wessex to carry a range of ordnance and additional equipment.

The carriers, which consisted of a forward and aft spar and a faired-over beam assembly housing the electromechanical release unit (EMRU), switch box and crutches, were bolted to a support arm protruding through the side of the cabin bottom structure and braced with struts to brackets on the fuselage. Fusing units

BELOW Mk 11 depth charge fitted to the port weapons carrier on Wessex HAS Mk.3 XP142. *(Author)*

bombs and 3.5lb smoke/flame floats. It also allowed for the installation of the 97-gallon long-range external fuel tank.

The armament stores carried were fused and released by the Observer using airborne presetter controls in the cabin. These presetters were also used to set the initial search depth and floor depths of the torpedoes while a manual-release handle in the cockpit allowed the pilot to jettison any of the stores in an emergency.

Armament platform

A pair of light alloy box-structure armament platforms could be mounted, one on either side of the aircraft, positioned over both mainwheels and bolted and braced to the fuselage by a pair of struts and beams.

On each platform could be installed a forward-firing machine gun while a pair of shafts protruding horizontally from the assembly at the front and rear allowed the carriage of two SS.11 wire-guided surface-to-surface or air-to-surface missiles, rocket projectile (RP) launching pods containing up to 28 per side and/or a smoke grenade discharger.

Angled plates provided the ordnance being carried with some protection from the hot engine exhaust gases. These heat shields could

ABOVE A Wessex HAS Mk.1 dropping depth charges.
(via Nick Blackman)

bolted to the outside of the front and aft spars allowed stores to be fused while a parachute pack slide was fitted at the rear.

Stores capable of being carried included Mk.30, 43 and 44 torpedoes, submarine (Clevite) simulator, the Mk.11 depth charge and 600lb nuclear bomb as well as the Mk.12 light series carrier, which allowed the carriage of smaller items such as the 25lb smoke and flash

RIGHT Wessex HU Mk.5 XT482 ('Q/CU') of 707 NAS firing a salvo of RPs on the Castlemartin Ranges.
(Author's collection)

be manually hinged upwards to improve ground clearance for moving the aircraft around.

SS.11 missiles

The Wessex could carry up to four SS.11 anti-tank missiles, each of which had a range of 1,640–10,000ft.

AS.12 missiles

Special 'Boitier' fixed light alloy pylon and launcher units could also be fitted to the weapon carriers to allow AS.12 wire-guided air-to-surface missiles to be carried outboard of the mainwheels. Curved, light alloy guards were fitted over the upper half of the wheels in this configuration to prevent the tyres from being damaged by the hot efflux from the missile's rocket motors when fired.

Control of the missiles was via a joystick on a T.10.K control unit mounted in the cockpit on a tray held in place on struts with quick-release pins such that it was held above the interseat console. A switch box fitted at the forward end of the overhead switch panel allowed the missile stores to be selected or jettisoned individually or all at once. A wire cutter was also activated from the panel, severing the guidance wire between the aircraft and the missile being fired.

Guided weapon sight

To aim the SS.11 and AS.12 missiles, the M.260 guided weapon sight is installed within a circular bezel in a modified panel fitted in the port side cockpit roof above the second pilot's seat which replaces the usual clear Perspex panel. The unit comprises a gyro-stabilised head which protrudes above the canopy frame and optical assemblies housed within a vertical telescopic case within the cockpit.

By looking through binocular eyepieces, the operator can control the sight head through 30° up or down and 27° left to right using a stick on the controller assembly mounted on a tubular framework above the interseat console. The 22° field of view is produced at 2.5× magnification for the initial launch of the missile which can be increased to 10× magnification for the guided run in to the target.

The sight can also be used in conjunction with a simulator unit for training purposes. Here, a spot of light is generated and shone into the sight to imitate a moving missile. When the flight time of the missile has expired, the spot of light stops moving, briefly becoming brighter to simulate the missile exploding, before extinguishing.

Nuclear depth charge

From the early 1970s, the Wessex HAS Mk.3 was also configured to be able to carry the WE.177A 600lb nuclear anti-submarine depth charge on the port weapon carrier. This device measured some 9ft in length and was capable of yields between

ABOVE Wessex HU Mk.5 XT761 ('VU-B') of 848 NAS with SS.11, AS.12, forward-firing machine gun and torpedo fitted. Both cabin windows have also been removed. *(Author's collection)*

ABOVE Wessex HAS Mk.3 XS862 ('650/PO') of 737 NAS takes off from RNAS Portland with an inert WE.177A 600lb MC nuclear depth charge fitted to the port weapons carrier. *(Author's collection)*

protect from enemy small-arms fire was the fuel computer within the nose.

Machine guns

Depending on variant, the Wessex could be armed with two types of 7.62mm general-purpose machine gun (GPMG) installations: a fixed, forward-facing pair and a pair of pintle-mounted guns in the cabin.

Forward-firing machine gun

The forward-firing GPMGs were standard service-issue items quickly modified to fit on to the lightweight armament platforms. Because of their proximity to the engine exhausts, light alloy heat shields were fitted over the gun breeches and feed chutes to protect them from hot engine efflux. They were belt-fed from stainless steel ammunition boxes, each containing up to 500 rounds, fitted by quick-release pins between the fuselage and the platforms with spent cartridge cases and links being ejected via chutes through holes cut into the platforms themselves.

There were two methods of 'aiming' the guns: in one, the first pilot was provided with a 'ring-and-bead' sight, the ring being mounted inside the front windscreen and capable of being flipped rearwards into a stowed position when not in use, while the bead was mounted on a tubular support frame on the outside of the windscreen. The second was via an electrically operated Mk.1 reflector sight bolted to the underside of a platform mounted in front of the pilot between two of the cockpit frames. An adjustable, hinged screen displayed the reflected aiming graticule, allowing the pilot to aim the guns or, if fitted, rocket projectiles. An opposite-hand reflector sight could also be fitted to the second pilot's position if required.

General-purpose machine gun

With the HAS Mk.3, the aft left and right escape hatches, cabin door, Observer's and Sonar Operator's seats and marine marker stowages could be removed to allow two pintle-mounted

0.5 and 10 kilotonnes, depending upon the depth of water in which it was being dropped.

Armour plating

Armoured plates could be fitted, one immediately underneath each cockpit seat pan, and a panel at the bottom corner of each side windscreen. A hinged panel on the outboard side of both pilots was designed to hinge outwards to allow the pilots to get in and out and could also be jettisoned in an emergency. As well as the cockpit occupants, one other item deemed to be sufficiently important to

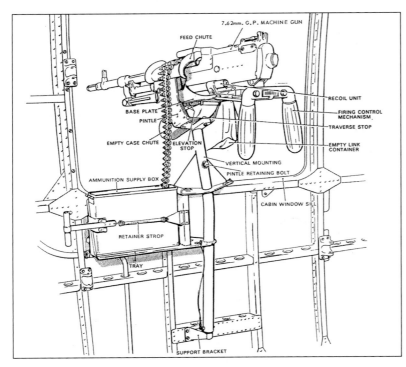

LEFT Pintle-mounted GPMG fitted with the port cabin window removed. *(AP101C-0105)*

7.62mm GPMGs to be fitted, firing through the respective window aperture.

For the HU Mk.5, the two cabin GPMGs were mounted on U-shaped pintle assemblies operated using twin-handled firing control grips by the cabin occupants. The starboard gun pintle was fitted on to a box structure gate mounting held in place on a pivot plate on the floor at the forward frame of the open cabin doorway and a fork fitting. This allowed it to be swung out and locked into any one of three firing positions and giving it an operating arc of 113°. An ammunition box was secured to this mounting by a bungee cord.

The port GPMG protruded through the cabin window aperture with the glazing having been removed. The pintle was mounted on top of a vertical bar secured to brackets on the window sill and side structure with rounds being fed from an ammunition box held into a stowage on the structure below the window by a bungee cord. A canvas bag collected the used links with the spent cartridge cases being ejected outboard and safely away from the aircraft.

Both GPMG assemblies had mechanical stops built in to prevent the guns from traversing into a position which could cause extremities of the aircraft such as rotor blades and undercarriage from being accidentally hit by bullets.

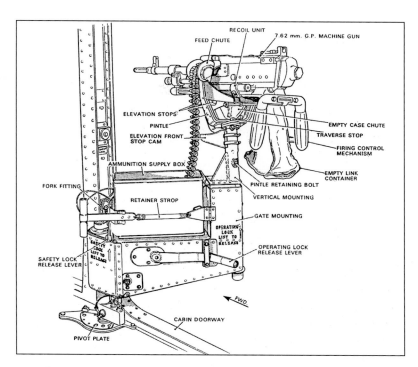

ABOVE GPMG fitted to the starboard cabin door forward structure. *(AP101C-0105)*

External loads

Four lugs were fitted to the underside of the aircraft, on to which the four 75cwt wire cables that comprised a sling arrangement could be fitted. This sling supported the cargo release unit – originally an EMRU, later superseded by a semi-automatic cargo-release

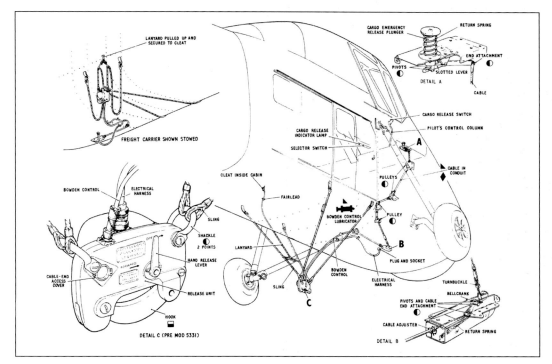

LEFT Details of the SACRU and underslung load arrangement. *(AP101C-0101)*

LEFT A Wessex HC Mk.2 of 28 (AC) Squadron approaches groundcrew to pick up an underslung load of barbed wire to reinforce the border between China and Hong Kong. *(via Jonathan Falconer)*

unit (SACRU) hook suspended under the fuselage. This hook allowed a 4,000lb external load to be carried at a maximum AUW of 13,300lb (HAS Mk.1) and at speeds not above 90kt. The hook was opened to release the load by the pilot using a release switch in the cockpit or by a switch in the cabin operated by the aircrewman. In the event of an emergency, however, the load could be jettisoned by the pilot using a foot-operated, sprung-loaded emergency release plunger on the cockpit floor.

When not in use, the sling arrangement could be pulled up and secured to the port side of the aircraft using a lanyard which routed in through the port side of the fuselage.

External hoist

Mounted on a tubular boom assembly on the outside of the aircraft immediately above the cabin door was the electrically controlled, hydraulically driven hoist, capable of lifting up to 600lb. Originally, the hoist used a 100ft long cable – this later being upgraded to 300ft – wound around a drum. The hydraulic motor was supplied with fluid via pipes which attached to self-sealing couplings on the fuselage. The hoist could be operated either by the first pilot using a three-position switch on the collective lever handle, or by the aircrewman using a similar switch arrangement fitted above the cabin door. In an emergency, the cable could be severed by an electrically fired, cartridge-operated cutting mechanism through which the cable passed. Guarded switches to operate the system were installed in the first pilot's cyclic stick and above the cabin door.

Heave-ho hoist

In lieu of the external hoist, a basic 'heave-ho' hoist frame could be fitted using the same

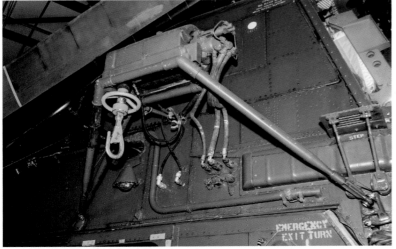

LEFT External hydraulically operated, electrically controlled winch fitted above the cabin. *(Author)*

RIGHT A mainwheel flotation bag and the tailcone bags are all that are stopping Wessex HAS Mk.1 XM871 from going to a watery grave in the Red Sea, 21 August 1975. Meanwhile, the crew await rescue in their life rafts. *(Author's collection)*

RIGHT A mainwheel flotation bag and the tailcone bags are all that are stopping Wessex HAS Mk.1 XM871 from going to a watery grave in the Red Sea, 21 August 1975. Meanwhile, the crew await rescue in their life rafts. *(Author's collection)*

attachment points. Although designed to take weights of up to 300lb, a strengthened frame allowed loads of up to 750lb with a 'swarming' rope of between 110ft and 160ft for the rapid disembarkation of troops while the aircraft was in a hover of between 20 and 30ft.

Emergency flotation equipment

When helicopters are operated over large expanses of sea, the potential for engine failure leading to a ditching in the water is ever present. In the event of that happening, the aircraft will almost inevitably capsize and quickly sink. To give the crew the maximum opportunity to vacate the aircraft safely, and also to try to keep the aircraft buoyant in order to allow it to be recovered, the Wessex had two types of flotation equipment: flotation canisters and flotation bags.

Tailcone floats

Situated within the tailcone was a permanently inflated float consisting of three non-connected, neoprene-coated bags, 8ft long, 3ft high and 2.5ft wide at the forward end and tapering to match the profile of the tailcone. The float assembly, pressurised to 35psi, was secured in place by six thin ropes laced through eyelets.

Mainwheel floats

Each mainwheel could be fitted with its own flotation canister. These canisters were attached to steel tubes which slid through the hollow wheel hub and were secured in place with a quick-release pip pin. Each canister had its own cool gas generator, igniter and submersion

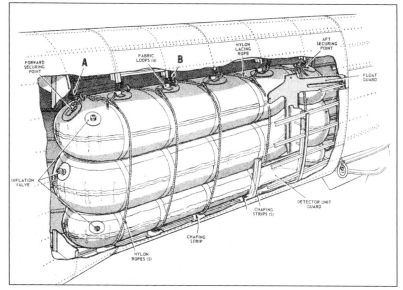

ABOVE Tailcone flotation bag arrangement. *(AP101C-0101)*

RIGHT Wessex HAS Mk.1 XP110 ('776/PO') of 737 NAS showing the original canister-type flotation equipment fitted to the main undercarriage oleo. *(Author's collection)*

actuator mounted on to a bracket on the
undercarriage strut inboard of the wheel.

When the submersion actuator came into
contact with salt water with a minimum salinity
of 3%, the igniter was automatically fired,
causing the generators to produce gas to
inflate the flotation bags neatly packed inside
their canister cover. As the bags expanded,
the covers would blow off, allowing the bags to
inflate to their full size.

The mainwheel floats could be operated
manually by the pilot from the cockpit in the
event of the aircraft landing in fresh water which
would not trigger the submersion actuator.

Engines

The Wessex in its different guises was
powered by two different types of gas
turbine engines: the Napier Gazelle Mk.161 of

the HAS Mk.1, Mk.162 of the HAS Mk.31 and
Mk.165 of the HAS Mk.3/HAS Mk.31B variants,
and the Rolls-Royce (née de Havilland/Bristol
Siddeley) Gnome (in various marks) of the HC
Mk.2, HCC Mk.4 and HU Mk.5.

Napier Gazelle Mk.161 and 165

The Napier Gazelle NGa.13 Mk.161 turboshaft
engine fitted to the Wessex HAS Mk.1, Mk.162
of the HAS Mk.31 and NGa.18 Mk.165 of the
HAS Mk.3 and HAS Mk.31B variants comprised
an 11-stage axial compressor which delivered
air to six combustion chambers positioned
around its outer casing.

The compressor itself was driven by the
hot combustion gases turning a two-stage
turbine which differed from other variants of the
engine in being a mirror image in order to turn
the same way as the Wessex's main rotor. A
mechanically separate single-stage free power
turbine at the rear drove the output shaft to
the main rotor gearbox via epicyclic gearing,
producing 1,450shp and 1,600shp respectively.

Installation

As per the original Sikorsky piston-engined
installation, the British gas turbine engine was
fitted in the nose at an angle of approximately
35° to the horizontal. The Gazelle had, uniquely
for the time, been designed specifically to allow
angular or vertical installation. Two tubular
side support struts and a triangular lower strut
attached to hardpoints in the nose supported
the front end of the engine, while horizontal

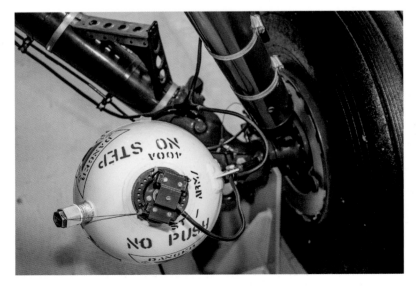

OPPOSITE Napier Gazelle Mk.165. (AP101C-0103)

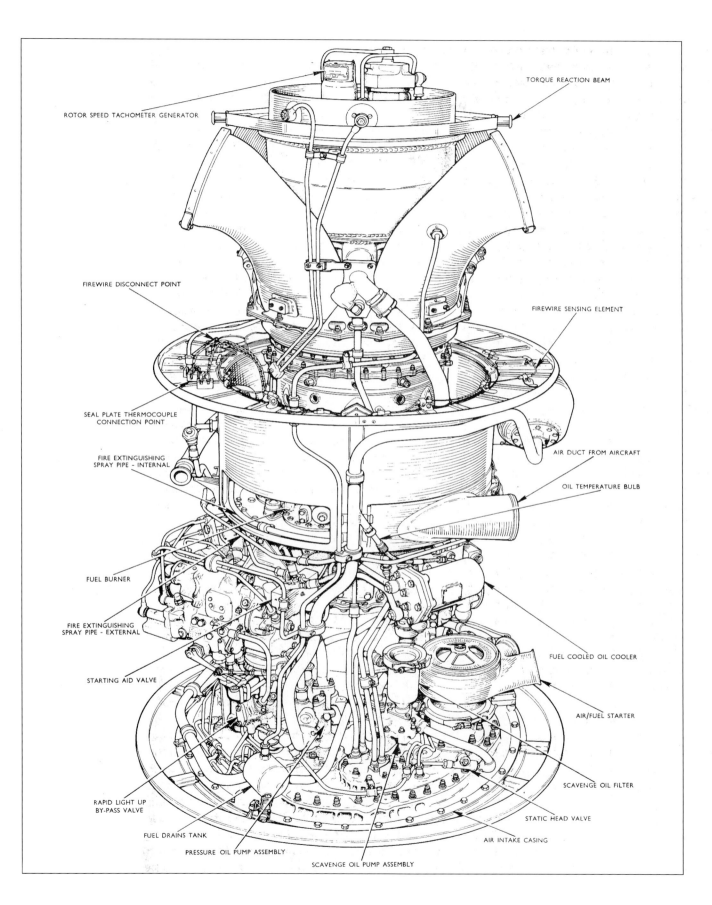

ROTOR SPEED TACHOMETER GENERATOR

TORQUE REACTION BEAM

FIREWIRE DISCONNECT POINT

FIREWIRE SENSING ELEMENT

SEAL PLATE THERMOCOUPLE
CONNECTION POINT

FIRE EXTINGUISHING
SPRAY PIPE - INTERNAL

AIR DUCT FROM AIRCRAFT

OIL TEMPERATURE BULB

FUEL BURNER

FIRE EXTINGUISHING
SPRAY PIPE - EXTERNAL

FUEL COOLED OIL COOLER

STARTING AID VALVE

AIR/FUEL STARTER

SCAVENGE OIL FILTER

RAPID LIGHT UP
BY-PASS VALVE

STATIC HEAD VALVE

FUEL DRAINS TANK

AIR INTAKE CASING

PRESSURE OIL PUMP ASSEMBLY

SCAVENGE OIL PUMP ASSEMBLY

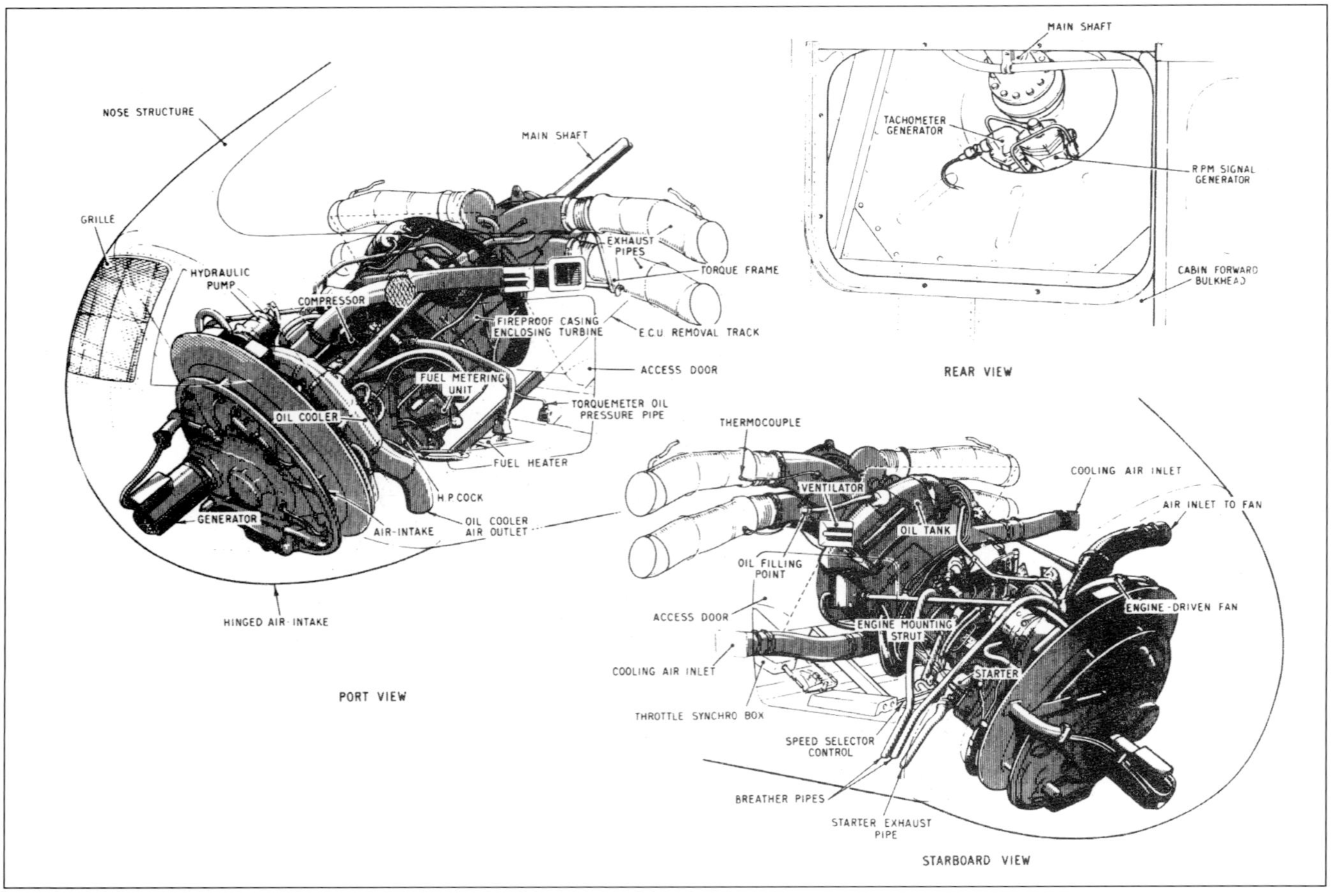
NOSE STRUCTURE
MAIN SHAFT
GRILLE
HYDRAULIC PUMP
COMPRESSOR
EXHAUST PIPES
TORQUE FRAME
FIREPROOF CASING ENCLOSING TURBINE
E.C.U. REMOVAL TRACK
ACCESS DOOR
FUEL METERING UNIT
TORQUEMETER OIL PRESSURE PIPE
OIL COOLER
FUEL HEATER
H.P. COCK
GENERATOR
AIR-INTAKE
OIL COOLER AIR OUTLET
HINGED AIR-INTAKE
PORT VIEW
MAIN SHAFT
TACHOMETER GENERATOR
R.P.M. SIGNAL GENERATOR
CABIN FORWARD BULKHEAD
REAR VIEW
THERMOCOUPLE
COOLING AIR INLET
VENTILATOR
AIR INLET TO FAN
OIL TANK
OIL FILLING POINT
ENGINE-DRIVEN FAN
ACCESS DOOR
ENGINE MOUNTING STRUT
COOLING AIR INLET
STARTER
THROTTLE SYNCHRO BOX
SPEED SELECTOR CONTROL
BREATHER PIPES
STARTER EXHAUST PIPE
STARBOARD VIEW

ABOVE Installation of the Napier Gazelle Mk.161 engine in a Wessex HAS Mk.1. *(AP101C-0101)*

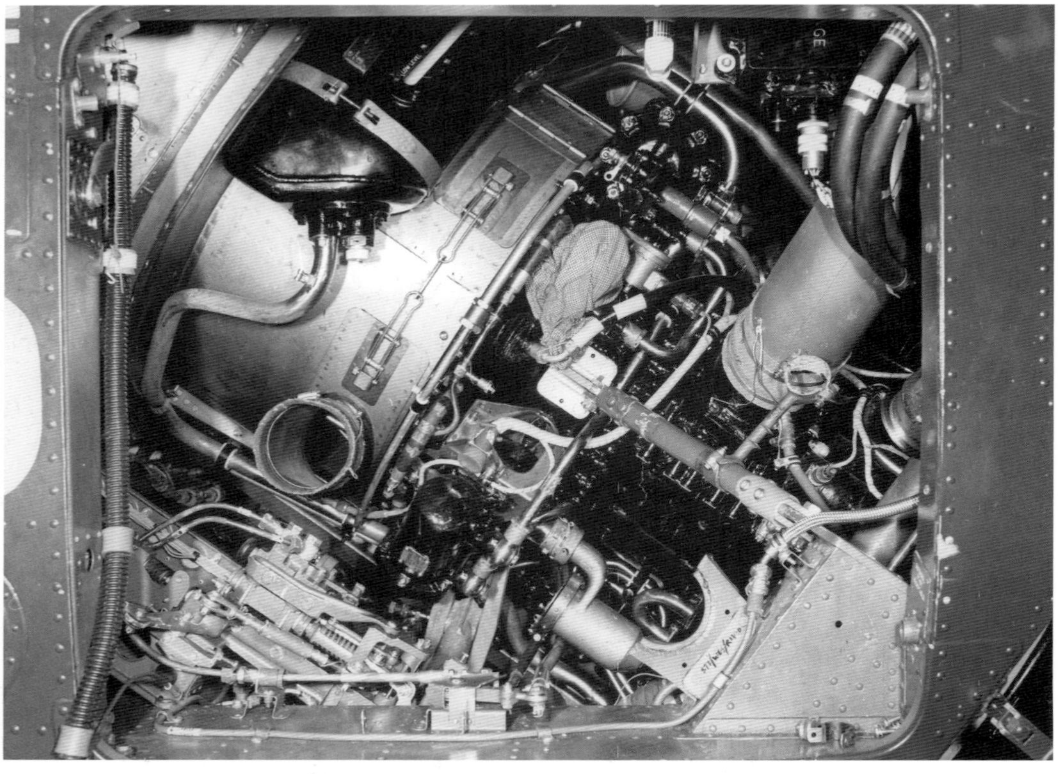

RIGHT View of the Gazelle engine through the starboard access door. *(Leonardo Helicopters)*

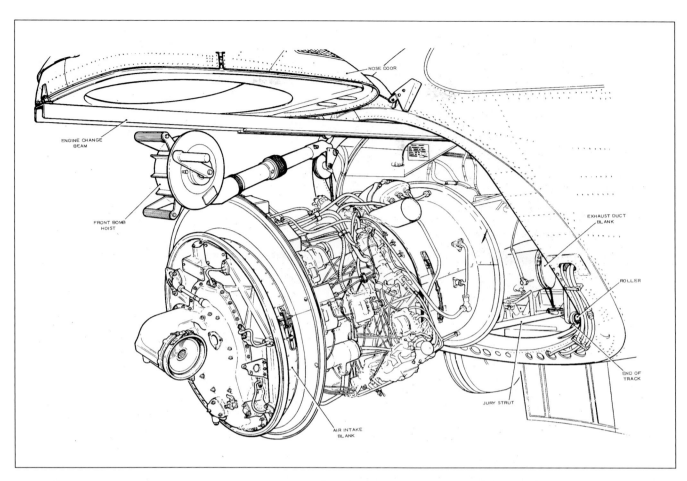

ENGINE CHANGE
BEAM

NOSE DOOR

FRONT BOMB
HOIST

EXHAUST DUCT
BLANK

ROLLER

END OF
TRACK

JURY STRUT

AIR INTAKE
BLANK

pintles from the torque plate fitted to the rear of the engine were supported on two vertical arms which formed a torque frame. At the lower end of each side of this frame were rollers which engaged with two inclined tracks on the engine bay floor. With the help of a removable engine change beam in the roof of the engine bay, and two standard mechanical bomb hoists – one positioned at the forward end and one aft – the rear of the engine could be rolled up and down the tracks, pivoting about the front, in and out of position as it did so.

Exhausts

Twin exhaust pipes attached to the bifurcated ducts protruded through both sides of the engine bay. An inner casing in each pipe with a gap in between caused a venturi effect, helping to draw exhaust gases through. On the outer lip a guard ring was installed to prevent the main-wheel flotation bags from coming into contact with the hot exhaust pipes in the event of them being activated.

ABOVE Installation and removal of a Napier Gazelle engine. *(AP101C-0103)*

BELOW Double exhaust arrangement of the Napier Gazelle on a Wessex HAS Mk.1. The rings around their edge were to prevent the mainwheel flotation bags from coming into contact with the hot exhaust in the event of them being inflated. *(Author)*

LEFT IPN tank filler point and starter cartridge firing head on a Wessex HAS Mk.1. *(Author)*

Engine starting system

As with many similar gas turbine engines of the era, the Gazelle Mk.161 engine was started using a combination of an explosive cordite cartridge and a highly volatile liquid propellant fuel turbo-starting system. A starter breech fitted to the right-hand side of the engine and accessible via a hinged panel above the engine starboard access door carried three explosive cartridges, rather like

BELOW Installation details of the Rolls-Royce Gnome engines. *(AP101C-0105)*

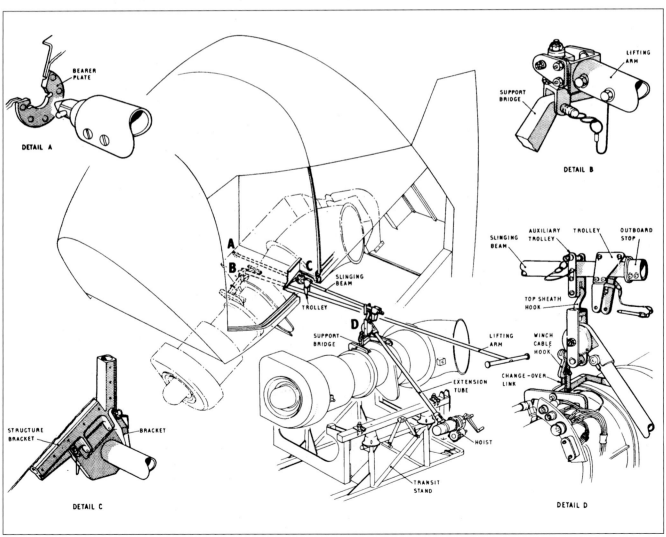

IPN/AVPIN

Isopropyl nitrate, known variously as IPN and AVPIN, was a highly flammable monofuel which burnt with a barely visible flame and was used in gas turbine engines fitted to both fixed- and rotary-wing aircraft types throughout the 1950s and through to the 1970s. It did have a poor reputation, however, due to many accidents where the pipes within the starter systems became blocked. The resultant release of high-pressure air would then cause a huge explosion, followed by fire which would often consume the magnesium alloy airframes in a fierce and uncontrollable conflagration.

ABOVE Starter firing head in the open position showing two of three cartridges fitted. *(Author)*

those of a shotgun. When electrically initiated via a master switch on the cockpit overhead panel, these cartridges would fire into a reaction chamber where the heat and pressure increase would cause approximately 2.5 pints of isopropyl nitrate (IPN, otherwise known as AVPIN) to be fed into the breech from a header tank, itself holding up to 12.25 pints, where it would rapidly burn in a controlled manner. The high-pressure gases generated by this reaction would then be fed into a turbo starter unit mounted on the front of the engine which would then turn the compressor over sufficiently to allow its own internal ignition sequence to establish.

A stowage box with hinged lid was fitted to the structure inside the cabin just aft of the door capable of holding up to three IPN system starter cartridges in spring clips.

The sides of the engine were accessible via doors either side of the nose (which also doubled as access steps), the hinged nose air intake at the front and panels underneath.

With the Gazelle Mk.165 of the HAS Mk.3, the IPN starter was replaced by a Rotax turbo air starter. This system had two ways of being operated: internally or externally. With internal start, fuel pumped to a combustor from the aircraft's fuel system was mixed with compressed air from two spherical bottles mounted in the mouth of the air intake at between 1,350 and 3,000psi, and the

explosive mixture detonated. The hot gases produced would then turn the turbo starter attached to the engine via an engaging box.

Wherever possible, however, the engine was started using an external Palouste ground air starter unit which fed low-pressure (20–48psi), high-volume air into the starter to turn it over, this time without the need for fuel or combustion.

Rolls-Royce Gnome Mk.112 and Mk.113

The two Rolls-Royce (originally de Havilland H1400, then Bristol Siddeley) Gnome free power turbine (FPT) engines were mounted side by side in the redesigned nose area of the HC Mk.2, HCC Mk.4 and HU Mk.5 variants. Although basically identical to each other, they were 'dressed' so that certain accessories could fit around the engine and for others to be accessible when the engine was installed. This meant that they were 'handed': Mk.112 being fitted on the port side and Mk.113 on the starboard.

Similar to the single Napier Gazelle, the Gnomes were both fitted on an incline – 34° 36' to be precise – but their installation was symmetrical about the aircraft's centreline and separated by a longitudinal titanium firewall, and removal was via the side instead of the front. Each engine bay was then subdivided into areas to segregate the compressor and turbine

OPPOSITE TOP **Port Gnome engine with structural support struts in position. The curved tank (left) contains oil for the coupling gearbox.** *(Author)*

OPPOSITE BOTTOM **Starboard Gnome engine installation in a Wessex HU Mk.5.** *(Author)*

areas by a transverse heat shield that encircled the two engines. Special heatproof blankets protected the coupling gearbox and the area above the engines.

Gas generator

The Gnome gas generator had a ten-stage axial-flow compressor consisting of steel blades fitted to a spinning rotor. These blades intermeshed with fixed stator blades attached to the inside of the compressor casing. Each pair of these rotor and stator blades was called a stage.

As air entered the intake it was drawn through the first three stages that comprised 38 inlet guide vanes (IGVs) and corresponding fixed stators. These aerofoil-shaped IGV blades were pivot-mounted, the angle of attack – the angle at which they met the airflow – of each being controlled by the engine control system's hydraulic actuator, fed by a tiny bleed of high-pressure fuel from the engine (via small control rods on the outside of the compressor casing) to manage the optimum airflow into the engine in varying rotational speeds and atmospheric conditions. Stages 4 to 9 comprised rotor and stator blades that progressively compressed the air as it travelled through.

The final stage – Stage 10 – was made up of exit guide vanes (EGVs) that directed the high-pressure air into the annular combustion chamber. Here the compressed air was sprayed with fuel and the highly combustible mix ignited.

This burning process caused the air inside to rapidly increase in velocity and temperature, giving it sufficient energy to turn the blades on the two-stage axial-flow gas generator turbine. With the two components linked together by a common shaft running fore and aft, the rotating turbine now effectively drove the compressor, thus making it a self-sustaining cycle.

LEFT **Gnome engine exhaust on a Wessex HCC Mk.4. Note the fuel filler point with lockable cover.** *(Author)*

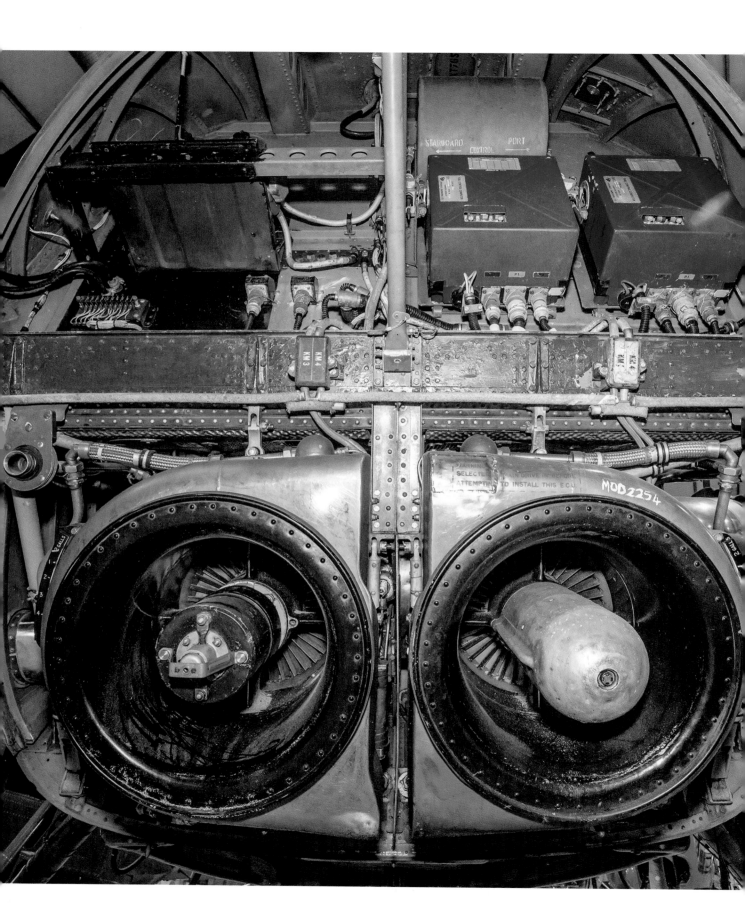

OPPOSITE View of the front of the Gnome engines, the starboard bullet fairing has been removed to show the electric starter motor. The engine oil tanks are fitted around the air intake assembly. Above the port engine can be seen the two fuel computers in their blue boxes, while above the starboard engine is the battery position. *(Author)*

Free power turbine

Installed immediately aft of the gas generator's turbine but operating independently (*ie* it was not connected mechanically to the moving parts of the engine), the FPT disc was driven purely by the kinetic energy of the hot gases from the gas generator impinging on its blades.

Coupling gearbox

In the Gnome-powered variants the engines were coupled together via freewheel units to a coupling gearbox mounted at the rear of the engines in between the two exhausts. This gearbox, the installation and removal of which was also achieved from the side, had accessory drives to run the electrical generators, coupling gearbox oil cooler fan, pressure and scavenge oil pumps, secondary system hydraulic pump for the flying controls and the two dual tachometers. The output from the gearbox drove, via an expansion coupling, the inclined connecting driveshaft which was connected to, and in turn drove, the MRGB.

The gearbox was supplied with oil, using gearbox-driven pressure and scavenge pumps, from a light alloy tank mounted in a cradle assembly on the starboard side of the forward face of the engine compartment rear bulkhead.

Fire protection

The fire protection system on all Wessex variants was essentially the same, consisting of two main parts: a detection system and an extinguishing system. Lengths of firewire sensing elements were positioned strategically around the engine bay, exhaust and fireproof casing which enclosed the turbine. Made up of thin stainless steel outer tubes with an electrode running through its centre and insulated from the outer material by a special filler, the decrease in electrical impedance of

the electrode of the firewire caused by a rise in temperature as a result of fire triggered a warning system in the cockpit.

For the Gazelle-powered aircraft, a single extinguisher bottle was mounted on the port side of the engine bay just inside the access door. This was connected to a pair of spray rings: one encircling the engine compressor and the other surrounding the turbine within the fireproof casing.

On the Gnome-powered variants, two extinguisher bottles were positioned on the sloping bulkhead in the electrical compartment in the nose immediately forward of the windscreen: one on the port side and one on the starboard. Stainless steel pipes ran forward from the bottles and down through the compartment flooring into the engine bay to four spray nozzles – one each side below the compressor section and one each side above the turbine section – to engulf the area around the engine with fire-suppressing chemicals.

In the event of a crash-landing, both extinguisher bottles would be fired by a pair of inertia-sensitive switches within the nose, set to activate at 4.5G.

Fuel computers

Mounted on the forward face of the forward bulkhead in the nose were the two blue-coloured boxes which housed the Gnome engine fuel computers, themselves operated by inputs from the engine control box.

BELOW Air intake scoops and sprung-loaded doors allowed access to fight engine fires with extinguishers while on the ground. *(Author)*

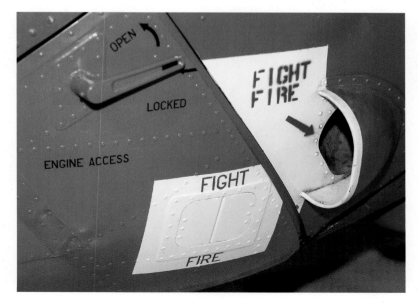

Chapter Nine
Flying the Wessex

The Wessex, in all of its guises, was well loved by those who flew it. With its AFCS and the power benefits of the gas turbine it was a step change in comparison with its predecessors. Its rugged construction made it the perfect choice for conducting flying operations even in the most inhospitable of environments.

OPPOSITE No. 845 NAS Wessex XT470 ('(Y)L/H') making a hasty retreat from a mock battle scenario during training. *(via Jonathan Falconer)*

In 1970, straight from initial helicopter training on the diminutive Hiller HT.2 at RNAS Culdrose, John Beattie found himself transferred to 707 NAS to begin learning to fly the Wessex HU Mk.5 – a helicopter that he, like so many others, would soon come to love.

The ground school syllabus on the Wessex took the inevitable two weeks to complete, courtesy as ever of Harry Willis and Colin Steer at Culdrose. It was our first brush with a 'computer' to control the engine, albeit a fairly basic 'mixing box' would probably describe it better; it certainly had very limited capabilities compared with the computers of today. It had eight inputs and one throttle output and did the job remarkably well, keeping the rotor rpm exactly right, when it was minded to work. Practising computer freezes did seem to take up a lot of our training time though and understanding the low- and high-power overspeed trips on the engine added a degree of mystique to the whole shebang. The auto stabilisation equipment (ASE) was also a bit of an intricate deal to get your head round, with anticipators, closed loops and follow-up circuits, but we all got there in the end.

We had a locally produced simulator to help learn the checks. Nothing like the high-definition visual, full motion jobs of the new millennium, but looking for all the world like a Mk.5's cockpit and with dials and switches that worked, due to the hard graft and diligence of a few gifted local

technicians. We sat for hours learning check lists by rote, which was the order of the day for a single-pilot aeroplane.

Then it was time to tackle the real thing, big and shiny sat out there on the pan in a warlike 'sand and spinach' colour scheme, although about that time all were being refinished in all over green starting with the frontline squadrons. My instructor was an excellent ex-Royal Marine pilot, Paul Brown, who had just remustered into the RN and unusually held the rank of Sub Lieutenant.

The course consisted of various modules, general flying practice, instrument flying, navigational exercises (navex) at medium and low level, formation, mountain flying, night flying, load lifting, RP firing and machine gunning, troop drills, deck landings and so on. With the inexperience of youth on our side we managed okay, despite only having about 90 hours total on the Hiller and Whirlwind HAS Mk.7 at the start of our course with 705 NAS. The instructors were excellent and took some pains to ensure that we understood all we should and yet at the same time ensured we achieved the right standards. I must say there was a low-flying navex occasion where 'do what I say and not copy what I do' was the order of the day!

So how did we fly it? The initial walk-round was fairly standard, ensuring the flotation cans were pip-pinned securely in place, the HF aerials were complete, nothing hanging off, the tail wheel locked (the locking pin could break), open the big engine air intake door to ensure nothing in the intakes and closure secure when it was shut again.

Clambering up the outside was pretty easy though the uninitiated always seemed to make a fuss about it. Lift down the servicing platform and clamber up on to the rotor gearbox area. On the rotor blades ensure the BIM indicators showed white. These kept a pressure of gas in the blade spar and a leak indicated a crack or some-such with the BIM now showing black. On the rotor head, the flapping restraints and droop stops looked sound and of course all blade wrist and taper pins secure, particularly important as we tended to fold the blades all the time. The oil cooler was fed with air by a belt-driven fan and you checked that these belts were in good order and taut. Gearbox levels checked and the absence of any spills or leaks; these might not necessarily be a problem, but you needed to know if more had been generated during your flight which might indicate a problem developing. Clamber down, shutting the platform securely on the way. The cockpit side window was also the cockpit door and quite large. It could be kept open in warm weather of course but firmly closed in the Arctic!

Having got in, standard left to right checks around the cockpit were carried out to establish full and free movement of all controls, knobs and levers, setting the various switches in the correct position to start and dials showing the correct ambient readings. The main drive was exercised by selecting the starboard speed select lever (SSL) forward and port SSL back, listening to the drive moving and checking the magnetic indicator, then reselecting 'ACC' drive for start (you could do a single engine ferry flight if urgent, but then had to start with no hydraulics, which meant clamping the stick firmly between your legs until sufficient pressure built up to offload the high stick forces). Select the port engine on the start master and press the button for 3 seconds, operating an electromechanical timer, which engaged the electric starter motor and spun up the compressor. Once 4,000–5,000rpm was showing, the HP cock was selected to open, waiting until the engine lit and ran up to 14,500rpm all on its own. Once running, the rpm was eased up to 180–200rpm equivalent. Now, checks were made to ensure that the secondary hydraulics and generators were online and the controls cycled to ensure that the blades moved full and free. The start master switch was flicked to 'Stbd' and, having checked that the rotor brake really was on (310lb on the pressure gauge) the start button was pressed again. With the HP fuel cock selected ON, the starboard engine would then run up to 14,500rpm. The pilot would now seek and receive a 'permission to start' signal from the (hopefully) attentive marshaller stood out in front of the aircraft.

The starboard SSL would now be eased up to give 600–700lb of torque and the rotor brake would be released slowly. As soon as the blades started turning, the starboard SSL was advanced to accelerate the rotor smartly but smoothly by setting 350lb/hr fuel flow. The Wessex was

particularly prone to ground resonance, especially if the tyre pressures were a bit down or the undercarriage oleos a bit soft, aided perhaps by a gust or two of wind to get things started off. This could get a little hairy on the forward spots of the flight deck in gusty weather, but the aircraft was tied down securely of course.

Engaging the rotor

To start the rotor, the rotor brake was first selected to OFF. To prevent shock loading of the system, this needed to be slowly to start with, allowing one or two full revolutions before quickly releasing the brake altogether and allowing the rotor to increase speed rapidly. This would help to prevent any tendency for 'padding' to set in which could lead to ground resonance.

With the rotor now running at its normal 233rpm, the port engine SSL was brought fully back before selecting the main drive switch. Getting this bit wrong could be very expensive! With the main drive engaged and port SSL fully

BELOW A Wessex HU Mk.5 of 847 NAS preparing to lift a Sioux AH Mk.1 of 3 CBAS Royal Marines from HMS *Intrepid*. *(via John Beattie)*

forward, the starboard SSL was also back to ensure the port engine had engaged properly by noting rotor rpm was being maintained solely on the port engine. The starboard engine SSL was now advanced once more and you were ready to go through the after-start checks. Further checks were, of course, necessary depending on your mission: pre-take off, winch, load hook, weapons, etc.

Taxiing

With the parking brake selected to OFF, the tailwheel would be unlocked, the AFCS also switched off and the rotor set at 220rpm, followed by the cyclic stick being carefully eased forward to tilt the rotor disc. At the same time, the collective lever was also raised slightly to generate lift. Combined with the angle of the rotor disc, the aircraft would now begin to move forward.

To manoeuvre the aircraft on the ground, the rudder pedals were operated: right rudder pedal forwards to turn right and left pedal forward to turn left.

Taxiing speed was controlled purely by the amount of collective input with the cyclic remaining in the same position throughout. To stop the aircraft, initially to check that the wheel brakes were working correctly, the collective would be lowered fully, the wheel brakes applied and the cyclic stick allowed to return to a neutral position.

Once taxiing was complete, and before take-off, the aircraft was allowed to roll a few feet forward to allow the tailwheel to align fore and aft before the tailwheel lock was engaged.

Take-off

As the collective lever was raised, so the torque reaction of the main rotor would cause the aircraft to naturally yaw to the right. To counter this and keep the aircraft pointing straight ahead, some left rudder pedal input would be required. While the aircraft sat in a low hover, the cockpit instruments would be checked to ensure that all temperatures and pressures were safely within limits.

Transition to forward flight

By combining forward cyclic stick and an increase in collective input, the aircraft was transitioned from a hover into forward flight,

quickly accelerating to 55kt to begin the climb and increasing to the optimum 65kt giving a rate of climb of between 1,800ft per minute at 1,000ft and 1,100ft per minute at 8,000ft.

Transition to the hover

As with the climb, the optimum speed for the transition from forward flight to the hover was 65kt at a descent rate of 500ft per minute. As the speed reduced to 30kt, the aircraft was flared by gradually pulling back on the cyclic stick to tilt the main rotor disc while simultaneously pulling up on the collective lever to increase pitch (and, therefore, increase lift), accompanied by a gradual increase in left rudder pedal to counter the increased torque, slowing the aircraft and bringing it to a stable hover.

Landing

The Wessex was usually landed in a nose-up attitude with the tailwheel making contact with the ground first before the collective lever was lowered to bring the mainwheels down on to the ground. Due to the way in which the aircraft hovered one wheel low, the port main-wheel would touch down first, followed by the starboard. With the collective lever fully lowered, the tailwheel lock was disengaged and the aircraft taxied back to dispersal.

We all got used to the Wessex very quickly and found it a delight to fly, both visually and on instruments, with or without the help of the ASE. Engine-off landings were very easy and we practised them a lot until two instructors got it wrong one day in about 1974 and crashed at Merryfield. The grown-ups decided that we were hurting more aeroplanes practising than due to real malfunctions, and a double engine failure was very unlikely anyway so engine-off landings were banned. We continued to practise autorotations of course, just stopped doing it with engines at idle power. I did get to do a couple more years later when I was a 'trapper', attempting to discover how quickly the rotor rpm got to the minimum when engines failed. This followed the fatal crash of a Wessex HAS Mk.3, where the pilot didn't get the collective lever down quickly enough and the rotor didn't get into autorotation. When they get to a certain low rpm, nothing you do will speed them up again and a crash is inevitable. The other favourite exercise was single or double computer freezes. If a computer froze, which they were apt to do now and then, that engine's power output was stuck at whatever power was set when it happened. The computer was turned off and, when ready to land, the SSL was retarded and the computer turned back on, at which stage the engine would run back to idle. If not, the engine would be shut down using the HP fuel cock. Needless to say, if you were in flight this may not be ideal and practising to get the aircraft to a position where you could run the affected engine down to idle was a regular exercise.

A double failure was more difficult and you probably had to end up doing an engines-off landing. I don't recall any double failures for real but did have a couple of actual single failures in my 1,500 hours on the type.

The fuel computers could be affected by a damp night out in a field somewhere causing a failure to start and on one occasion I had an anti-icing air pipe seal fail, blowing hot air directly on to the computer sending it haywire, causing me to switch it off and land on one engine.

The other Wessex problem was a 'runaway' engine, either up or down. If going up with the rotor rpm increasing you had to stop the high engine, while limiting the rotor rpm to below 258 and then quickly lower the collective lever to avoid the good engine running up to maintain the high power demand and probably cause its overspeed trip to operate, giving you no engines!

A runaway down was only a problem if you needed very high power, perhaps hovering with a heavy load. The single-engined performance was extremely good, but you couldn't quite do everything on one that two could give you. The response of the engines was generally very good and cases of having to deal with rotor droop were few and far between. If the revs did droop, the disc became less efficient and you got a lot less lift for the power you were applying, but that would usually only be on one engine. With both engines running you could easily apply more power than the gearbox could

BELOW Making an impromptu tent around the starboard engine to help warm the engines prior to starting in the cold wastes of Norway. *(David Baston)*

cope with. Our normal maximum power was 3,200lb/ft of torque, with 3,520lb/ft available transiently. As a very young Sub Lieutenant, at night with my Commanding Officer flying, he pulled to 4,500lb/ft, which caused all sorts of maintenance checks to be done and ultimately rejection of the gearbox. Needless to say, I didn't tell him off!

Flying characteristics were pretty good and we soon got to being able to fly accurately and carry out exercises like zero-zero landings with ease, simulating being at a high all-up weight and operating in high temperature environments where a hover wasn't possible ... using the energy in the flare to kill both forward speed and rate of descent at the same moment to achieve a landing, perhaps rolling the tailwheel along a little. Running landings were easy and used a lot less power. For take-offs in such conditions, 'cushion creep' or running along to about 20kt did the trick if the terrain allowed it. The ASE was a 'stability augmentation device' and not a full-authority autopilot. It did make life easier, but we flew quite a lot with it off to maintain our basic skills.

Manoeuvrability was good and we spent some time practising fighter evasion, usually against Hawker Hunter 'attackers' and latterly Sea Harriers. The key to our survival was seeing the attacker before he could line up for a shot at us, so four pairs of eyes had their search sectors and yelled if they saw a bogey. Putting the aircraft into a crossing rate on the attacker's line was one tactic, making him continue to turn. Getting out of the line of sight by hiding behind trees, houses, etc., was fairly important too. Climbing prior to a rapid descent was another tactic, causing the attacker to have to bunt. Racking the aircraft round the corners low level is exhilarating flying, especially when you know the attacker hasn't really got any bullets! Diving down valleys and stopping quickly before shooting off in another direction was all very confusing for the fighter pilot.

The Wessex was a fairly easy aircraft to fly on instruments with the ASE, but only slightly less so without the ASE engaged and we spent hours practising this facet, carrying out various exercises with a full and 'partial' panel of instruments. Indeed, great satisfaction could be derived from flying accurately using

only air speed indicator, altimeter, compass and the turn and slip ball. Quite difficult at first but with a little practice easier and the knock-on effects were immense; indeed that early ability has saved my bacon a couple of times over the past 47 years in other types, I am sure. We also practised self let-downs through cloud and Ground (Radar) Controlled Approaches. Needless to say, the term 'Grub Navy' was coined to describe how we liked to operate down among the weeds, as in any operational theatre there wasn't likely to be much radar and we wouldn't be familiar with the terrain, so staying under the cloud as long as possible gave us the best chance of achieving our objective.

The armament was pretty basic, mounted on two stub wing attachments carrying fixed forward-firing .303 machine guns, which were prone to jamming, aided by door- and window-mounted machine guns. However, provided purely for the pilot's amusement were 2in rockets in pods of 14 on each stub wing. The pods wobbled a bit so were never going to be too accurate, and the sight was the standby sight used in the Blackburn Buccaneer fixed-wing strike aircraft, but fitted slightly out of the direct line of the pilot's vision! Most of us used a chinagraph pencil cross marked on the inside of the windscreen as a sight. To be fair, a few pilots did get reasonable results on the range, but most of us found it an 'area' weapon and wouldn't have hit a truck or tank with any consistency. The rocket itself had a solid motor which quickly got it to supersonic speed but then free fell most of its flight. The head was a relatively small explosive good for only light armour or soft vehicles.

We could carry a FFR (fitted for radio) Land Rover, weighing some 3,100lb underslung or any lesser load, normal Rovers being about 2,900lb. When the 'light' gun came into use in the early 1970s replacing the howitzer, it wasn't light enough and we had to lift it in two pieces.

Seating was provided for 16 troops, but seat number 16 was never used (I still don't know why), though our normal load was 12 equipped Royal Marines. They would usually have Bergens full of the stuff that Marines carry, which we had a standard weight for. However, occasionally we would weigh the Bergens and discover that

they were considerably heavier than we had been allowing for. Marines didn't like to run out of water, food, ammunition, etc! The deal with Marines was to be the initial strike force in any conflict and to that end they needed to get as many men and equipment on the ground as possible in the first assault, followed by a rapid succession of support sorties. Hence, we would try to get as many of our 20 aircraft on the first wave as we could. However, 16 would be a good number to rely on. The first wave would probably be troops who would establish a beachhead or landing site in the area of operations. We would then race back and forwards bringing the field guns, more troops, vehicles, trailers, ammunition, water and so on. In HMS Albion, we had 750 troops and a battery of guns plus their supporting vehicles and equipment. They could all be on the shore inside four hours (obviously, dependent on distance ship to shore). We beat the USS Guadalcanal in the Mediterranean by hours, they using CH46s, a far more capable helicopter. HMS Albion had nine normal operating landing spots, but by juggling, 12 aircraft could be spotted on deck and launch for an assault. The other four would be manned and ready to start port engines the second they came up on the lift. Maintenance crews would spread the blades on the lift (makes it easier) and troops embark, taking little more than a few minutes to catch up with the rest. It was a very slick operation by all concerned.

Assaults could be carried out at night as well and the aircraft were later fitted with Beta lights on the spine and rotor blade tips so that we could formate much easier. I remember starting without the Beta lights and it was pretty hard work. No NVG in those days. I only did one 16-ship assault at night, to landing sites in Malaya. Rather than fly in formation we departed one minute apart and flew accurate speeds and headings. Well, that was the theory anyway and I'm pleased we only tried it the once! As a fall-back, anyone could yell 'lights' and we'd all put on our anti-collision lights. Someone did and we expected to see a nice single file of light leading to the landing site, but it was more like a Christmas tree, lights everywhere. We continued practising night formation in smaller numbers after that.

Lifting underslung loads was a bit of an art that we revelled in. Getting your aircraft over the load in the right place quickly and hooked on without lots of mucking about involved teamwork between you and the aircrewman – likewise arriving at the site and putting the load down smoothly and quickly and then getting out of the way was very satisfying. I do have to admit that the odd Land Rover did get hurt now and again. Occasionally a load would misbehave, usually something light like a Wombat anti-tank gun: just a pipe on a pair of wheels really. If they started swinging, there were several things you could do: turn, speed up, slow down, climb or descend. Usually the way you flew had an effect on the load and you could fly in sympathy with it . . . or not. Ultimately, you didn't want it swinging too far and hitting the rotor blades, so you could dump it with the quick-release button on the pilot's stick. The Marines didn't like that.

Putting the troops where they wanted was sometimes tricky and mountain flying skills were often used. On one occasion I was asked to hover on one wheel on a very narrow track on the spine of a ridge while the Gurkhas hopped out from the cabin. All went well and I was about to lift when one chap clambered back in all flustered and the aircrewman yelled at me to hold position. It seemed the chap had dropped his bottle of rum out of the top of his pack and wasn't going anywhere without it!

Coping with the moods of the mountains was sometimes a bit of a challenge, success all being down to being able to read the various air currents. The Wessex was good in mountains because of its ample power reserve and good control response but also the pilot had to read the conditions well and spend time wind-finding. You could easily be going down rapidly with full power applied in a downdraught or climbing fast but with the collective lever fully down in an updraught. Leaving yourself a get-out clause or escape route was also part of survival. Needless to say, as you got higher things did get trickier, or more to the point, loads had to get lighter with altitude.

The Sea King HC Mk.4 came along in 1979 and slowly took over the Junglie role, ultimately acquitting itself extremely well. However, it lacked some of the characteristics of the dear old Wessex and was much less of a pilot's aeroplane . . . in my opinion.

OPPOSITE Wessex HU Mk.5 XT456 ('VA/B') of 846 NAS lifting a lightweight Land Rover from the deck of HMS *Bulwark*, July 1979.
(Author's collection)

Chapter Ten

Maintaining the Wessex

No Wessex could ever get airborne, of course, without the hard work of the maintainers, groundcrew and organisations set up to support the aircraft and keep it airworthy. Fighting against salt-laden atmospheres and maintaining the aircraft in anything from the freezing conditions of Norway to the stifling heat and humidity of the Far East, often far from proper engineering facilities, the aircraft would eventually return to the UK where specialist deep maintenance facilities could breathe new life into tired, often bent and broken airframes.

OPPOSITE Former 78 Squadron Wessex HC Mk.2 XR500 ('A') in the main airframe jig in F Shop at RNAY Fleetlands in 1971 with a mix of Wessex HAS Mk.1s and HAS Mk.3s in the background. *(RNAY Fleetlands)*

ABOVE Former 820 NAS Wessex HAS Mk.1 XS120 ('066/E'), complete with the squadron's stylised flying fish motif, in storage at the Fleetlands Helicopter Holding Unit at RNAS Lee-on-Solent in 1970. *(A.W.M. Groth)*

RNAY Fleetlands

The main bulk of the third- and fourth-line work undertaken on the British military versions of the Wessex was conducted at the civilian-manned RNAY Fleetlands in Gosport, Hampshire. Initially, this only extended to RN variants but, from 1967, aircraft from both the RN and RAF were worked on when the yard became responsible for tri-service helicopter maintenance.

With main airframe build jigs having been installed, Fleetlands had the ability to carry out the complete rebuild of aircraft that would otherwise have been written off long after the original production lines had ceased to exist. The yard boasted some of the finest facilities in the industry, allowing all manner of work to be carried out on site, including component overhaul, sheet metal repairs, plating, engine overhauls and full surface refinishing.

During the early 1970s, Fleetlands also used a hangar at nearby RNAS Lee-on-Solent as an overspill Helicopter Holding Unit, such was the volume of work, with the aircraft often being towed by road between the two locations.

The last Wessex to undergo scheduled maintenance at Fleetlands was XS508 in February 1986, but the HCC Mk.4s of the Queen's Flight continued to be flown in and out to have their high-gloss paint finishes refreshed right up until shortly before the Flight was disbanded and the aircraft retired.

In 1997, Fleetlands also played host to most of the final examples of the RAF's Wessex when the aircraft of SARTU, 60 and 72 Squadrons were all flown in on their last flights for long-term storage pending eventual disposal.

Wroughton

There were two units at Wroughton, near Swindon: the RAF's 15 Maintenance Unit, which took delivery of many of the early aircraft straight from the factory and both prepared them for service or for shipment via other units for overseas operations, and the Royal Navy's RNAY. The latter focused mainly on carrying out storage and modification work in conjunction with that being carried out at Fleetlands.

SAREW

With the advent of the Search and Rescue Wing (SARW) forming at RAF Finningley in 1976, a dedicated second-line servicing facility was also set up at the base for all RAF SAR Wessex and Whirlwind major maintenance: the SAR Engineering Wing (SAREW). RAF Finningley finally closed in December 1992 with the SARW disbanding at the same time.

Helicopter Maintenance Flight (HMF)

With the closure of SAREW, the maintenance of the RAF's SAR fleet of Wessex (and Sea Kings) transferred to the HMF at RAF St Mawgan, Cornwall, and remained there until the type's retirement.

Wessex Servicing Flight

The Wessex Servicing Flight was based at RAF Benson from 1980 until being subsumed within 72 Squadron in April 1982.

OILS, FUELS AND LUBRICANTS

Standard fuels:	AVTUR/FSII (F34), AVTAG/FSII (F40), AVCAT (F44)	
Alternative fuels:	AVTUR (F35)	Not to be used at fuel temperatures below +5°C in flight.
	AVTAG (F45)	
Starter fuel:	AVPIN (S-746)	
Engine:	OX38 (O-149)	
Coupling gearbox, MRGB, IGB & TRGB:	OX38 (O-149)	
Hydraulics:	OM15	Undercarriage shock absorbers, hydraulic system, rotor brake, hoist
Washer fluid:	AL11	
Windscreen de-icing:	AL8	

Aircraft Servicing Flight

While the Wessex HAR Mk.2s of the SAR fleet were maintained by SAREW and HMF and the 28 (AC) Squadron aircraft by HAECO, those of CFS/2FTS and both 60 and 72 Squadrons came under the contractor-operated Aircraft Servicing Flight at RAF Shawbury throughout the 1990s until the type's retirement. Detachments of personnel also undertook work on the 84 Squadron aircraft in Cyprus.

BELOW Maintainers carrying out main rotor blade tracking on Wessex HAR Mk.2 XR504. Each blade tip was marked with a coloured chalk and as they struck the canvas flag their prescribed path would allow adjustments to be made. *(Pete Wendes)*

Having previously worked on the Napier Gazelle-engined Bristol Belvedere, former RAF engine fitter David Barrow left the services and joined Bristow Helicopters Ltd (BHL), initially on the Westland Whirlwind. In 1974, however, he volunteered to become the Chief Engineer for Bristow's operation for Shell Oil in Port Harcourt, Nigeria, which at that time were flying the Wessex Mk.60.

The work for Shell consisted of flying people and freight to the offshore and swamp oil rigs in the Rivers State Delta region. It was not uncommon to have the state governor request a helicopter to do an election tour in the morning (white covers and VIP trim), do a midday run with an internal load of 50-gallon drums of lubricating oil and then return to collect the governor again in the evening. This sort of work, combined with the sun and tropical rain, played havoc with the aircraft's appearance but we were still expected to maintain a high standard.

We were also tasked with search and rescue and MEDEVAC work. As can probably be imagined, there was an alarmingly high accident rate in the Nigerian oil fields.

The Mk.60 was fitted, for overseas operations, with a different type of engine intake sand filter manufactured by Aviation Traders. Although these ugly-looking

ABOVE One of the hangars at HAECO, Hong Kong, with Wessex HAS Mk.1s of 845 NAS having their unit badges reapplied after receiving their new 'sand and spinach' camouflage, November 1964. *(HAECO)*

HAECO

While the main rotor gearboxes were still overhauled by Westland at Yeovil, the Wessex HC Mk.2s of 28 (AC) Squadron were supported almost entirely independently from the UK by the Hong Kong Aircraft Engineering Company (HAECO). The warm salty waters of the South China Sea surrounding the colony played even more havoc with the magnesium alloy structure than usual and some aircraft were known to require almost total re-skinning of the fuselage in an attempt to rid the airframes of corrosion.

RIGHT Ex-RN Wessex HU Mk.5 XS506 being stripped for spares at Aircraft Servicing Flight at RAF Shawbury on 10 May 1991. This was one of several ex-RN aircraft that were earmarked for a proposed Royal Auxiliary Air Force squadron to support the Territorial Army before the plans were abandoned. *(Tony Jupp)*

installations featured improved particle separators, they were incredibly heavy and used to wear their mounting hinges out regularly and we still had engines that were damaged by foreign objects.

Unlike its military siblings, the Mk.60 did not feature the UHF radios, nor a sophisticated autopilot system. It did, however, have the same SAS motors, powered by the Ferranti FAS A2W Stability Augmentation System.

The living conditions in Port Harcourt were generally good with about 50 bungalows on a guarded compound complete with swimming pool and golf course. The work, however, was intense, with average 25°C heat and high humidity. The aircraft flew an average of 100 hours a month – high for a Wessex – and the resultant high rate of component changes and scheduled maintenance took some keeping up with.

We had two expatriate engineers for each of the two shifts, the rest of the work being undertaken by the locally employed Nigerian workforce who did all of the loading, washing and after-flight greasing. They weren't aircraft trained, but some were actually quite good and could be entrusted with more technical work such as filter changes.

Rotor blade erosion was a major problem in the tropical rain, the abrasive nature of which would result in us having to effect regular changes of leading edge erosion tape, often in the middle of a busy day's flying. We also had a problem at Port Harcourt with fruit bats. These curious creatures, which had a wing span of around 12in, would fly down to the mangrove swamps to feed every morning before returning to roost at night. The sky would be black with thousands of them transiting to and fro and we would often hear a series of loud thumps as an unfortunate Wessex returning to base flew through these unavoidable swarms, heralding another evening of blade tape changing!

The red, white and blue paint scheme adopted by the Wessex Mk.60 – as with the rest of the BHL fleet – was introduced by Alan Bristow himself in the early 1970s and Shell hated it. They were worried that if an aircraft went down in the sea or the bush, no one would be able to see the uppermost blue colour. The 'old man' (as he was referred to by many of his employees) would not give in, however, so Shell insisted on having Day-Glo tape stuck on top which looked awful. Years later, I was working on an S-61 at Redhill when a girl appeared and got on board.

'What do you think of the new colour scheme?', she asked of me.

'It's a bit gaudy,' I replied.

'That's my father all over!'

Somehow I avoided getting fired!

PAINT SCHEMES

BS381C-110	Roundel Blue	All variants national markings
BS381C-172	Light Blue	84 Sqn UN markings
BS381C-218	Grass Green	781 NAS exterior
BS381C-241	Dark Green	2 FTS camouflage
BS381C-284	Mid Green	60 Sqn camouflage
BS381C-298	Olive Drab	HU Mk.5 exterior
BS381C-356	Golden Yellow	Emergency markings/upper fuselage/fuselage
BS381C-538	Cherry Red	Roundels/Danger markings/2 FTS markings
BS381C-629	Dark Camouflage	84 Sqn camouflage markings
BS381C-633	RAF Blue-Grey	Fuselage/transmission components
BS381C-637	Medium Sea Grey	Fuselage
BS381C-638	Dark Sea Grey	Interior, all marks/2 FTS camouflage
{	Black	National markings, stencils
	White	

Chapter Eleven

Wessex operations

Rugged and dependable, the Wessex in all of its variants was unquestionably a popular aircraft. Its relative simplicity, in the days before modern, complex computerised control systems, meant that it could be relied upon to operate effectively in all manner of remote, often inhospitable operational theatres, from the back of ships at sea or oil rigs, through to dense jungles and frozen Arctic wastes.

OPPOSITE Wessex HAS Mk.3 XP142 'Humphrey' of 737 NAS 100/HMS *Antrim* Flight operating off Grytviken, 1982. (Author's collection)

Ian Stanley

**Commander Ian Stanley DSO Royal Navy
began his operational career in 1969 as
a pilot flying the Wessex HAS Mk.1 with
829 NAS from the County-class destroyer
HMS *London*, later enjoying a period
on exchange with the Royal Australian
Navy before returning to see action in the
Falklands Conflict of 1982.**

I joined London Flight in Singapore and was
quickly put through my paces by the Flight
Commander to get me up to speed in the 'hot
and heavy' conditions. Night SAR circuits in
the Singapore Strait very quickly demonstrated
the poor old Wessex's engine limitations as we
tried to get into the hover using the FCS3 flight
control system. With cries of 'wind me down',
the second pilot wound down the radar height
hold as the Doppler system was reducing the
forward and lateral movement to zero. The
engine was limited to 19,600rpm and as we
approached the hover, the speed mounted,
sometimes reaching 19,300rpm just before the
FCS3 had managed to get the aircraft into the
hover. A very careful and coordinated winding
down was essential to capture the ground
cushion at the same time as we hit the hover.
Hunting for any semblance of wind was a
major issue!

Although the engine limitations were an
issue, the Gazelle Mk.161 also had a rather

unsettling problem with the connection of the
free power turbine at the rear of the engine
to the rotor reduction gearbox. There had
been several failures of the shaft, allowing the
free power turbine to overspeed and shed
blades. As the pilots were in effect sat on top
of the intermediate fuel tank and the shed
turbine blades prescribed their departure from
the engine through that tank, there had not
surprisingly been fatalities.

The instant solution to protecting the aircrew
was to surround the engine with a titanium
shield to contain the turbine blades and prevent
them from penetrating the tank. Although this
still left the unfortunate aircrew with an engine
failure situation, it was infinitely preferable!

Throughout HMS *London* Flight's
deployment to New Zealand, Australia, South
Africa and, finally, Puerto Rico, the aircraft was
on a five-hourly spectrographic oil analysis
programme (SOAP) sampling regime to detect
any early breakdown of the free power turbine
shaft before it became catastrophic. These
samples had to be flown back to the Naval
Aircraft Materials Laboratory at RNAY Fleetlands
in the UK for analysis, so when we got involved
in a SAR search in Tasmania over miles of bush
we were sending off samples after every flight to
get clearance for another few hours of flying.

As a weapon system, the Wessex HAS Mk.1
was the first night-capable ASW helicopter. The
FCS3 was a fixed-wing flight control system
adapted for helicopter use and, although
offering a quite exciting time in any sea state, it
did allow the aircraft to achieve a hover where
the Type 194 sonar ball could be winched
down into the water. With the sonar body fully
lowered, the FCS3 reference for the hover
was switched to a couple of sensors which
surrounded the cable as it passed through
the lower fuselage. As the cable became
deflected, it contacted these sensors, sending
signals to the FCS which would then move
the aircraft to maintain a steady hover over the
sonar ball. Height over the water was a rather
nervous comparison between the depth of the
ball and the overall cable length. This was a
rather immediate comparison in any sea state
and consequently needed monitoring and the
occasional intervention.

If established in an Anti-Submarine screen

ahead of the ships, the active sonar, although quite short on range, was a great deterrent. The ability to leave one 'dip' position on the screen and jump to another would come as something of a surprise to the submariner being hunted, suddenly finding that the helicopter had jumped to within range and, if carrying the right weapon, was about to press home an attack.

This process of 'jumping' was coordinated by the Observer at his station in the rear of the cabin with the aid of 'Jump cards'. These allowed him to direct the aircraft to the next required hover position, taking into account the climb-out from the hover and the next approach to the hover into wind. Once the sonar ball was raised out of the water the FCS was switched from 'Cable hover' to 'Doppler' and the automatic climb-out initiated. The aircraft flew itself to the next jump position with the sonar ball trailing on the cable beneath the aircraft.

During daylight, the jumping process could be quite quick, further complicating the submariner's attempt to achieve a firing solution against any surface vessel. The balancing act in these scenarios was always between fuel and weapons. A torpedo cost time on task but always dependent on the natural wind. The more wind, the easier the hover and therefore possibly a weapon could be carried. It was never an issue in hot windless conditions! How much fuel was the significant factor.

Converting to the Wessex Mk.3

Conversion to the Wessex HAS Mk.3 followed my first tour and the joy of a quite sophisticated FCS 30 flight control system as well as the Type 195 Sonar with extended cable length. The radar offered unprecedented independence and added another sensor for submarine detection. The Gazelle Mk.165 engine was more powerful and had overcome all the problems of the free power turbine driveshaft.

It was always understood that the Wessex HAS Mk.3 was the test-bed for the systems that subsequently went into the Sea King. FCS 30 was a good system. Fed by better stabilising gyros, accelerometers and a more refined Doppler – as well as a smoothed radar altimeter input – it provided flying control commands which had an intrinsic redundancy. Primary and secondary actuators moved the aircraft controls

to achieve the desired flying profiles and all those inputs to the system were copied to the flight director within the artificial horizon.

Training sorties regularly and gradually degraded the system until the pilots were flying the dunking profiles using the flight director and the raw blind flying instruments. Maintaining the aircraft on the protecting ASW screen was certainly easier. Of all its benefits, I believe that the smoothed height system was the most reassuring. Hovering at 30ft at night over a fairly rough sea was made so much easier as the system averaged out the waves and maintained the aircraft in a steady hover. This was also important as the increased length of sonar cable was thinner and could be over-responsive to sea movement.

Despite the excellent systems and radar, the harsh fact was that there was only one engine! On two occasions the engine failed on me. The first as I was leaving the hover and had climbed to 200ft when the engine surged. This was caused by a breakdown of the airflow through the engine usually associated with the variable inlet guide vanes that had to adjust to the demand from the engine to present the right airflow to match the fuel input. In short, the engine stopped producing the drive to the FPT. We ditched about 10 miles south of Portland Bill and despite a couple of strain injuries to the Observers in the back of the aircraft, we all got out and were quickly picked up by the SAR aircraft.

BELOW The sorry-looking remains of Wessex HAS Mk.3 XS121 ('435/PO') being brought ashore at Portland by the salvage vessel *Kinbrace* after ditching with Ian Stanley on board. *(Author's collection)*

The second occasion occurred during instrument flying practice when, as the instructor, I had given the student a practice engine failure scenario. We were at about 3,000ft at the time and he was flying on instruments. Normally we would enter autorotation, turn the aircraft into the known wind and bring the air speed back to the minimum descent speed of about 40kt. Once stabilised, the instructor would allow the aircraft to descend to a simulated cloud base where the student would visually pick a field and then climb away at about 1,000ft. Unfortunately, as soon as the student lowered the collective lever to enter autorotation, the engine surged. Luckily enough we had enough height and a number of good fields to choose from so I took control, shut down the engine and carried out an engine-off landing.

After my tour in 737 NAS I didn't see the Wessex again until I had an exchange tour in Australia where the RAN was equipped with the Wessex HAS Mk.31B. It was a bit of a strange mix of old and new. It had an excellent sonar system in the form of the AQS 13B with about 1,200ft of cable, together with an interesting transponder system fitted above the cockpit that provided a transponder-only plot of units in the area. No radar!

On the other side of the equation it still had the old FCS3 flight control system. The RAN had Sea Kings at the time I was there, so the Wessex HAS Mk.31B was employed as a night SAR aircraft. I was training officer and after several exciting night training sorties where the FCS3 struggled to cope with the huge swells of the Tasman Sea, the RAN eventually decided that they would leave the night SAR task to the better-equipped Sea King.

On return to the UK, I became Senior Pilot of 771 NAS equipped with a mix of Wessex HAS Mk.1s and Wessex HU Mk.5s. Initially, the day SAR task was carried out by the former and the aircrewman training task by the latter. Eventually the squadron was completely equipped with the Wessex HU Mk.5.

For day SAR, the Wessex HU Mk.5 was quite a good solution as the twin Gnome engines produced enough power for all situations. The limiting factor was the torque limits on the combining gearbox. Because of the power available, the ability to use lots of tail rotor thrust to cope with the wind variables and topography of the Cornish coastline made it an effective SAR aircraft.

One of the more exciting SAR commitments that we accepted was to provide SAR to the British Grand Prix. Two Wessex were flown to Brands Hatch and landed in the middle of the circuit. As this was not a recognised naval task, the crew had to fend for themselves and were bunking down in the medical centre and enjoying the hospitality of the BMW corporate tent for food! The value of an on-call helicopter at these events was proven when there was a nasty crash in the vintage car race. The survivors of the crash were in the helicopter and whisked to a central London hospital within 10 minutes. There was also the opportunity to fly a small display routine for PR purposes. These deployments took place for another few years until commercial aviation concerns took over.

On completion of that tour it was back to the Wessex HAS Mk.3 of HMS *Antrim* Flight and what would probably be one of the most challenging periods of my flying career. For it was during this tour that the ship was involved in the recovery of South Georgia and subsequently the Falkland Islands themselves.

Fortuna Glacier

The story of the Fortuna Glacier rescue has been told many times. It had been decided that in order to recapture the old whaling station at Grytviken, an assault would be carried out from the most unlikely route in to maintain the element of surprise. This required the insertion of SAS troops high up on to the glacier by helicopter.

With the SAS and their equipment crammed into two Wessex HU Mk.5s of 845 NAS operating from RFA *Tidespring*, we set off in our Wessex HAS Mk.3, XP142 'Humphrey', to lead the formation, using our radar to grope our way through the rapidly deteriorating visibility high up to the top of the glacier. With the troops and kit dropped off we descended back down again and recovered to our respective ships thinking that the job was done. How wrong we were! The following day, after a very lumpy night at sea in storm-force conditions, we were tasked to recover the troops before they perished.

It is a true testament to the blind-flying

equipment in the aircraft and the continual crew training that we were able to once more fly up the face of Fortuna Glacier in a severe blizzard. With my gaze firmly locked on to the instruments and Sub Lieutenant Stewart Cooper alongside me, monitoring what he was doing as well as searching for visual cues through the windows, it was teamwork in much the same way as any ASW night flying sortie. In the back, the Observer, Lieutenant Chris Parry, probably experienced the biggest departure from the norm, trying to navigate the aircraft forward using the radar which had a blind arc immediately forward caused by bulk of the main rotor gearbox. Meanwhile, Petty Officer Aircrewman David 'Fitz' Fitzgerald was concentrating on the vertical view from the back and was giving a regular vocal readout of our proximity to the ground: very useful when flying in a complete whiteout over a crevasse-riven glacier! On the plus side, the cold wind had at least improved the single Gazelle engine's power output. Although the windspeed was fluctuating wildly, causing severe gusts from all directions, the aircraft coped.

The story of the visits to the glacier and the subsequent loss of the two Wessex HU Mk.5s in the whiteout conditions has been recounted before. But, from an aircraft and crew point of view, the differences between the Mk.3, the Mk.5 and the associated crewing could not be

better underlined by those events. Despite the fact that the Wessex HU Mk.5 crews were all Arctic-trained, the conditions were more than a single pilot and crewman could cope with. Without the reference point of the Wessex HAS Mk.3, the whiteout conditions caused them to lose all visual cues and crash in the snow one after the other, thankfully without any loss of life. With a crew of four and the much greater quality of instrumentation and sensors, the Wessex HAS Mk.3 in comparison was far better placed.

Having returned some of the survivors to RFA *Tidespring*, we launched once more and this time, by going high above the clouds, we amazingly managed to find a break right above the remaining survivors. Landing alongside the brightly coloured dinghy that they were sheltering in, we managed to get them all into the back of 'Humphrey'.

As the weather closed in again it became very clear that this would be the one and only chance to get them off the glacier that day. We were, with all 13 on board, verging on being 1,000lb overweight but the aircraft lifted without an over-torque, aided once again by the very cold and strong wind. Once off the glacier, the next problem we faced was to land safely back on the ship. Luckily enough, the wind was still quite strong and the forward motion of the ship generated even more, but even so the landing was a sliding arrival on the deck without establishing a hover. Amazingly, we even managed to get down without an over-torque.

Although the aircraft later collected a few shrapnel wounds in Falkland Sound during an Argentinian air attack, 'Humphrey' was repaired and soldiered on until we arrived back in the UK where it was retired with dignity to the Fleet Air Arm Museum at RNAS Yeovilton where she resides to this day. After a second tour of the South Atlantic with a new aircraft, I left HMS *Antrim* Flight for a Sea King conversion and command of 706 NAS.

Despite a couple of engine failures and some exciting times with the FCS3, I remember the aircraft fondly and it had not let me or the rest of the crew down at the most testing of times.

BELOW Wessex HC Mk.2 XV726 ('J') of 72 Squadron with the Mersey-class RNLI lifeboat 12-29 *Eleanor and Bryant Girling*. *(via Peter Bell)*

Peter Bell

Squadron Leader Peter Bell was the penultimate Wessex Flight Commander on the Royal Air Force's 72 Squadron in Northern Ireland between 1998 and 2000. Having previously conducted a tour on the unit as Qualified Helicopter Instructor, he found himself specialising in a role not often associated with the HC Mk.2s deployed in the province: SAR.

The geographic area of Northern Ireland was easily accessible by the Royal Navy's Sea Kings of HMS *Gannet* SAR Flight at Prestwick, Scotland, and, to a lesser extent, the Wessex and later the Sea Kings of 22 Squadron at RAF Valley, Anglesey. Under normal conditions, these two bases would have successfully covered the Province. As a comparison, the Lake District in England is a similar distance from RAF Boulmer and RAF Leconfield and, despite that area having a far greater number of incidents compared to Northern Ireland, was part of the area of cover for these two Sea King bases for many years.

Headquarters Northern Ireland (HQNI), however, did not permit daytime SAR operations by mainland assets within Northern Ireland and surrounding coastal waters. The mainland aircraft lacked a defensive suite (Missile Approach Warning System and Infra-Red jammer) and aircraft and crew weapons. Their crews were not trained in tactical flying and did not have an awareness of the threat level in specific areas.

There had been an ad hoc SAR capability since the arrival of 72 Squadron Wessex in Northern Ireland which had included the much-publicised evacuation of the Sealink Larne to Stranraer ferry, *Antrim Princess*, on 9 December 1983, drifting in 60mph winds towards rocks off the isle of Muck after a fire in the ship's main switchboard had led to her engines and steering becoming disabled. By the mid-1990s, however, the provision had become formal, with a dedicated aircraft and crew declared for SAR within the province and surrounding waters, with requests from the Coastguard and Royal Ulster Constabulary being coordinated by HQNI.

The base of operation was the RAF Support

Helicopter (SH) ramp at RAF Aldergrove – 'Violet 813' as it was referred to in the code of military helicopter sites of Northern Ireland – so the task assumed the name of '813 Standby'.

The crew was available in the Support Helicopter Force Northern Ireland (SHFNI) Operations building or nearby messes and launch times were similar to the 15 minutes required from mainland SAR Flights, though there was never a formal commitment to that.

The airframe used for SAR was a standard Wessex HC Mk.2 of the SH fleet, dedicated to the SAR task line for a period of time as the role required the fitting of a winch and a wet floor in the cabin. Troop seats were folded up out of the way and standard package of winching equipment – winchman safety equipment, strops, hi-lines and a stretcher – were left permanently in the aircraft. The Nite Sun mount was taken off and cockpit door armour removed for ease of crew emergency exit over water. The GPMG mount in the cabin was also removed. One major item of equipment that was missing, compared to the 22 Squadron SAR Wessex, was the main undercarriage-mounted flotation equipment. Decca was still fitted for over-water position fixing, though by 1995, 72 Squadron was becoming an early user of GPS in the form of a Trimble unit fitted on the cockpit coaming.

The crewing was different to mainland SAR Wessex. No. 22 Squadron manned their aircraft with a Pilot, Navigator (who would often be in the left-hand cockpit seat and then move 'downstairs' in flight to act as the winch operator) and an Air Load Master (ALM) as winchman. On more rare occasions, either non-pilot role could be filled by an Air Electronics specialist. On 72 Squadron SAR, as in all Northern Ireland ops by that time, there were always two individuals in the cockpit: a Pilot and either a second Pilot or Navigator. In the cabin, the winch was operated by a senior ALM. One of the great strengths of the 813 Standby was the experience of the crews; in no way was it merely a bunch of SH crews playing at SAR. All of the captains were either former 22 Squadron or 202 Squadron captains; the ALMs who operated the winch had multiple tours on mainland SAR Flights, some having been instructors at SARTU. Their main role had been as winchman, but 30% of their training had previously been focused on the winch-operating role. Their strong background on the lower end of the winch cable also made them excellent mentors to the young SH ALMs who acted as our winchmen.

All of these young men and women had already been through a basic course at SARTU as part of their ALM training. Most would go on in the future to become full-time SAR winchmen on Sea Kings.

It is probably good to emphasise at this point that none of the cockpit or rear crew manned the SAR aircraft as their only role in 72 Squadron. All of them carried out normal

ABOVE Wessex HC Mk.2 XV506 ('V') alongside a Hunt-class patrol ship (formerly mine countermeasures vessel) of the Northern Ireland Squadron during the final years of the aircraft's operation with 72 Squadron.
(via Peter Bell)

SH tasking as well; in fact, the SAR standby only accounted for about 20% of their allocated schedule. Roughly, only about a third of the squadron got involved in SAR. For those who were lucky enough to do so, that, plus the demanding tempo of day and night SH operations in Northern Ireland, pretty much carried out in all weather, meant that this period gave them possibly the most varied flying of their careers.

Training adhered to a syllabus very similar to that for the mainland flights, but covered daytime operations only and, of course, the Wessex did not have the all-weather capability of the Sea King (in practice that meant very low-visibility operation over the sea and coastline; the Sea King was no better or worse at crawling up mountain sides in the pouring rain and darkness than any previous helicopter). Crews practised mountain flying, winching to cliffs and confined areas in the mountains and the coast, winching off lifeboats, other small boats and large ships. Also, the ever present 'drum winching': a feature in any SAR syllabus, that gave the crew practice in coordinating hovering over the water with limited references and with the small object in the water unseen to the pilot.

The very nature of this training and the involvement with other agencies meant that 72 Squadron's large, still green-camouflaged, SAR Wessex became a close part of the emergency community in Northern Ireland and a very visible, positive contribution by the UK military to the community as a whole. Often a fast-moving Seacat ferry from the Galloway ports would enter Belfast Lough with a Wessex practising hovering and winchman transfers on its upper deck. Frequent exercises were set up with Portrush, Kilkeel and Strangford RNLI, Mourne Mountain Rescue and Coastguard cliff rescue teams in Ballycastle and Portrush. It has to be mentioned that many of the volunteers in these organisations were from communities not necessarily supportive of the British military presence in Northern Ireland, yet the relations with these teams were as good, if not better, than anything on the mainland. The squadron also had a SAR display crew, participating in several displays in coastal locations throughout each summer season.

David Paul

David Paul began his Fleet Air Arm flying career in July 1970 with the 'elementary' fixed-wing flying training stage on the Chipmunk, followed by the 'basic' rotary-wing stage on the Hiller and Whirlwind helicopters of 705 NAS at RNAS Culdrose. After this came the 'advanced' flying training on the Sea King HAS Mk.1, also at Culdrose, with 706 NAS before eventually moving to RNAS Portland for the 'operational' phase, this time on the Sea King HAS Mk.1 of 737 NAS.

During our time in 737 NAS we were invited to let the Aircrew Appointer know what our preferences were for our first operational squadrons. Having been trained 'up the creek and back again' by this stage, I was disappointed to be told that there were no vacancies in 826 NAS (HMS *Eagle*'s Sea King squadron) but that there was one as second pilot in HMS *Antrim*'s Wessex HAS Mk.3 Flight. And so I was to spend the next two months converting from the shiny new twin-engined Sea King to the much older, single-engined Wessex before joining the Flight in January 1972. It may have been disappointing at the time but with hindsight the wealth of experience I gained was well worth it.

One exciting part of the conversion was to do some engine-off landings and a group of us went up to RNAS Lee-on-Solent to be instructed by Ian Jones who was loaned from 706 NAS at Culdrose. The bulky sonar gear was removed to lighten the aircraft a bit and away we went. It was not as exacting as the Hiller (not like thistledown) or the Wasp (so I was told) but fun all the same and put to good use a few days later when Ian had a real engine failure with Maurice Fitzgerald in the Portland circuit and did a perfect engine-off landing into the harbour, not even getting wet but somehow managing to lose his aircrew watch in the process!

The first challenge after joining the Flight was to get proficient in the anti-submarine role and learn how to operate the Mk.3 properly. During three trips abroad, we operated in the Mediterranean twice and then had six months away in the Far East. It should have been nine months but I was flown home early for my next

appointment. Flight Commanders could either be Pilots or Observers; ours was John Neville-Rolfe, a Pilot, and he put me through my paces with a keen eye for detail and right amount of 'carrot and stick' to get my mind into handling the Wessex properly. As the aircraft could be flown single-pilot it also meant that once I was up to speed I could be sent off with the Flight Observer, Brian Rowley, and/or the Aircrewman, Jeff Heather, to gain more confidence on my own. It always had to be two pilots at night in the anti-submarine role, though. Leading Seaman Heather and I did a Vertrep (vertical replenishment) with an RFA vessel on one occasion and I thought it all went very well until they thanked me and said that they wouldn't charge me for the ensign staff! In fairness, they did have a very small deck and it was early on New Year's Day.

In February 1972, while we were in the Mediterranean, the Commander-in-Chief Western Fleet (Admiral Sir Edward Ashmore) was transferred to *Antrim* by a jackstay transfer. In case he should somehow end up in the water it was decided that we should be airborne as SAR. We stooged around at around 1,000ft above the proceedings and landed back on when the old man was safely aboard. The Flight Commander noticed some unusual vibrations during the flight (I didn't!) and had the aircraft checked after shutdown. One of the cotter pins which, after blade-spreading, was inserted to hold the main rotor blade in position on the main rotor head, had fractured and the bottom half, with its large locking 'safety pin', had dropped by about half an inch. Should the pin have been lost in flight it would have been us in the sea in a

mangled heap rather than the Admiral.

Apart from torpedoes, we could also be armed with the Mk.11 depth charge. These were very old stock at that time and we had the pleasure of dropping a couple which were life-expired. In action, they could be released from whatever height was required but for safety's sake in peacetime we had to drop from 500ft in case they detonated on hitting the surface. We each practised a couple of runs by dropping smoke floats on top of smoke floats before having a go with the real thing. After the depth charge had been released, a steep turn allowed us to follow the most satisfactory 50ft column of water after they exploded. In a later incarnation of *Antrim* Flight, the Flight's Observer, Chris Parry, recalled how straddling the Argentinian submarine *Santa Fe* with a pair of Mk.11s caused it to return alongside in South Georgia as quickly as possible with significant leaks. The AS.12 missile and Mk.46 torpedo attacks by other aircraft had little effect. Having personally watched a couple of Mk.11s explode, I certainly wouldn't like to have been in the *Santa Fe*!

Antrim's next deployment was to the Far East via South Africa, Kenya and three Red Sea ports. Despite fighting going on in Ethiopia at the time to try to force the country to grant Eritrea independence, we nonetheless flew the aircraft up to Asmara and back. Although only a flying distance of about 40 miles, Asmara sits at an altitude of about 8,000ft and to get there we had to follow a steep valley up into the mountains. We were initially torque limited, then power turbine inlet temperature (PTIT) limited, then finally N^1 (Ng) limited climbing at V_{broc} until

ABOVE Wessex HAS Mk.3 XS862 ('406/ AN') of 737 NAS HMS *Antrim* Flight picking up a shore party studying wildlife on Torishima in the Pacific Ocean, 5 May 1973. The aircraft wears a cartoon bulldog brandishing a large club. *(David Paul)*

we staggered over Asmara airfield at 8,500ft in a temperature of 25°C. The V_{min} and V_{max} were only separated by about 4kt and it felt as if the aircraft was balanced on a pinhead. The return to Massawa, sitting in 40°C heat, was virtually one long autorotation back down the valley and our temporary base on some scrubland near the dockyard.

There was some flying off Singapore when we reached it and it was fun to carry out radio checks on the long-range HF with the Wrens in the tower all the way back at Yeovilton. I often wondered if any of them checked up to see where 'Navair 406' was operating when we gave our position relative to Horsburgh Light off Singapore.

We carried out several naval gunfire support exercises in the Far East, the ship opening fire at a target ashore with her 4.5in guns and, once the first fall of shot was observed, we in the Wessex would give corrections to the ship to bring the shells on to the target. It was very satisfying when the shells started falling right around the target.

We also carried out a Casex with the Royal Thai Navy and one of their submarines. It was the real deal with high temperature, high humidity and a heavy aircraft, but in the dark and on a windless night. The technique was to set a slight nose-up attitude in the descent to 40ft to lower the sonar body, as the Doppler radar did not return any groundspeed information from the smooth sea. The height was taken care of by the RadAlt hold. Gradually, keeping the aircraft in balance and gently slowing down at 40ft, the downwash stirred up the sea enough to give a ground speed reading and the FCS hover could be re-engaged. The sonar body was lowered and the hover then controlled by pitch and roll detectors either side of the sonar cable. Gripping stuff.

While in transit, 'jumping' to our next dip position and looking for the Thai submarine, there was suddenly a very loud bang followed by continual thumping and airframe shaking. It is not original to say it but the cockpit really was filled with flying hands and adrenaline. It soon became obvious that we were still flying and the Observer saw by shining his torch outside that it was in fact the port flotation bag causing all of the racket. During maintenance earlier in the day, the two canisters containing

the bags had been opened and the bags checked, but during the repacking the securing-edge lugs of one canister had split. The crack should have been stop-drilled but wasn't and the containing can eventually fell off in flight, causing some mighty frights among us, the port torpedo carrier having also been broken half off.

After visits to Japan, South Korea and Thailand we eventually reached Hong Kong and the date for my flight home. I was pleased to see my relief at Kai Tak and after a chat and farewells to the Flight Commander and Observer I went off to the departure area and they went off into Hong Kong for a monumental 'haircut run' to get to know each other, getting back on board late and much the worse for wear.

It was back to the Sea King next for me. I had really enjoyed flying the Wessex HAS Mk.3 – a delight to handle and, despite its lack of endurance, a very versatile aircraft as the members of HMS *Antrim* and HMS *Glamorgan* Flights were later to prove 'down south' in 1982. I was, though, very happy to have two engines again when downwind at low level in a storm at night!

Mike Lehan

In 1978, after completing a total of twenty-two years in the Royal Navy, Mike Lehan took the decision to move to the other side of the world and transfer to the Royal Australian Navy. Although originally recruited as a Qualified Helicopter Instructor on their new Westland Sea Kings, initially he found himself unceremoniously sent to 'push paper' in Navy Office, Canberra, while the new aircraft's serviceability issues were ironed out.

In a very short space of time I was 'rescued' with the offer to go back to flying, not on the Sea King, but on the venerable Wessex HAS Mk.31B – basically a Royal Navy HAS Mk.3 but with a bigger engine – based at the Naval Air Station at Nowra, on the south coast of New South Wales.

And so, it was back to 'seat-of-the-pants' flying in the Wessex, a helicopter that I had flown almost continuously for 20 years: a factor that was later to save my life and that of my Observer.

As part of our familiarisation training, we were tasked to fly an inland navigation exercise along the Great Dividing Ridge, flying past Pigeon House Rock on the way back. Historically, this landmark was used by Captain Cook as a lead-in marker to enter Jervis Bay. At 2,500ft high it was a significant feature on the landscape.

During briefing we were informed that the Australian pilots had landed on the platform, just below the summit. What they failed to mention, however, was that they were flying the Bell Iroquois UH-1B of Vietnam fame, a helicopter with a much smaller skidded undercarriage.

It was a beautiful day with about 25kt of wind blowing in the range and we decided that we, too, would land on Pigeon House Rock.

Approaching the landing site, we conducted a high-level recce, followed by a low-level overshoot to check the landing area thoroughly. All textbook stuff.

Textbook, that is, until the landing itself.

Bringing the Wessex in, we hovered over the ledge where there was quite an updraught. It was extremely tight and I lowered the collective lever very cautiously. Because of the strong updraught, I did not need much power, and so down we settled. Just as I thought we were fully down, I noticed the rear fuel gauge needle starting to cycle. I knew, from experience, that this would only happen if there was air in the system . . . or a fuel leak. . . .

I immediately applied power, and needed every ounce available to get us off the rock. We shot up to 5,000ft where I levelled off. Suddenly we were completely shrouded in a fine fuel mist. The forward fuel gauge was rapidly going down, the rear one still cycling.

Training kicked in and I put the aircraft into autorotation, putting out a Mayday call and heading for the bush. Fortunately, we saw a clearing large enough to put the Wessex down in. We did a power landing and were just about to shut down when we ran out of fuel.

The duty SAR Iroquois helicopter arrived soon afterwards and I asked the pilot to fly me up to the landing ledge. As we approached it became all too clear what had led to our emergency. A 4ft, two-by-two 'Bus Stop' pole from Canberra City had been cemented into a wedge in the centre of the potential landing area, fixed in place by a troop of local

Boy Scouts who had taken it up the rock as an evolution. The pole had blended into the granite-type rock face, making it difficult to see.

Back at the emergency landing site, we inspected the underside of the Wessex. The pole had pushed up and cracked the high-pressure fuel pipe leading directly to the engine. Had the pipe completely severed, the end result may not have been as good. Thank goodness for sturdy British engineering!

The poor Wessex was lifted out beneath an obliging Chinook and was soon flying again.

Not exactly a good start to my flying career with the Royal Australian Navy. However, those who flew the Wessex would no doubt vouch for how sturdy and forgiving she was, allowing many of us to fly another day.

Tony Stafford

Previously having flown the Wessex HAS Mk.1 with 815 NAS aboard HMS *Ark Royal* and 820 NAS aboard HMS *Eagle* between 1963 and 1968, Tony Stafford left the Royal Navy for 'Civvy Street', joining Bristow Helicopters in 1969 initially on the Whirlwind Series 3 before converting to the Wessex Mk.60 and a 7,500-mile transit flight in G-AWOX from Gatwick to Phuket lasting 20 days and 76 flying hours.

After almost two months of idleness in Singapore it was back to flying and a totally new experience. Our task was to fly all of the drilling rig components, supplies and men from site to site in the Sumatran jungle. The maximum load that the Wessex could carry on the hook slung underneath it was 4,600lb. So every bit of the rig had to be dismantled to be less than that figure.

It was a daunting task, for the whole rig including the accommodation portakabins was about 1,700 loads. Added to that figure were all of the drilling pipes and other consumables needed to operate the drilling programme; altogether, over 3,000 trips.

We were based in a hangar by the side of a large river in Djambi, a city in the centre of Sumatra. The river was used to transport all of the materials to the closest point to the rig site. A team of locals led by a wiry little Frenchman (ex-Foreign Legion) went by foot into the jungle and cleared a big enough site for us to hover the helicopter in with more labourers. The area was then cleared so that we had enough space for all of the equipment to be brought in by underslung loads. Our first rig site was 32km from the river, quite a bit further than we had been advised, and because of the extra fuel we needed, flying the loads out was particularly demanding as the two poor old Gnome engines struggled to provide enough power.

The aircraft were flying ten hours a day, virtually continuously. We flew with just one pilot doing about two and a half hours at a

go, followed by a similarly long break. After a fortnight on the operation we flew back to Singapore for a week's rest. It was really hard work, but very satisfying to see the rig grow in the middle of virgin jungle. In a way, it was also sad to see modern industrial demands spoil such untouchable countryside.

Occasionally, we took the recce crew up river for them to walk into the jungle to find the next site. I remember once landing by a small village and waiting for an hour or two while the oil crew discussed a new rig location with the local headman. It was obvious that none of the villagers had ever seen a helicopter before. Very gradually they approached us, terribly afraid that it might attack them, and then they began to touch it and run away just in case it bit them. Before long, they were rubbing their bodies along the fuselage as though the magic would flow into them! At this point we got rather worried that 50 or so natives would start damaging the aircraft so we had to drive them away to a safer distance. It was quite an experience.

However, on Monday 13 March (and lucky not to be a Friday), my bubble burst. I was flying a load of fuel drums back to the main rig site on my own, but with a couple of local lads in the cabin. The drums were in a net underneath the helicopter. For a week or so, we had noticed that this particular aircraft was a bit juddery, particularly feeling a vibration through the rudder pedals. The engineers had checked it out and found no mechanical problems, and we thought it might just be dust getting into some of the controls and giving a little roughness, but not dangerous.

In fact, as I had only found quite recently, during a maintenance overhaul undertaken a couple of weeks before, a bonding strip had been incorrectly fitted over a rubber coupling joint on the tail rotor driveshaft. So on this occasion, as I pulled power to hover over the large fuel dump to drop my load, the shaft snapped and the helicopter, very suddenly and violently, began to turn. I was in an awful situation. I couldn't climb away and I dare not land on top of 150 drums of kerosene. We continued to rotate, getting quicker and quicker. All the people working at the rig site had now heard the whining and clatter of the engines and knew something awful was happening.

RIGHT Captain Tony Stafford. *(Tony Stafford)*

After some 25 turns, I saw we had moved a few yards away from the dump, and decided that I had to get the Wessex down.

With heart in mouth, I pushed down the collective lever and with an enormous crash and judder, the four main rotor blades tore into the tree trunks and debris around us. Amazingly, the aircraft stayed upright, probably held there by the load underneath that I had unsuccessfully tried to jettison. Even more luckily, nothing had exploded and there was no fire.

A bevy of very energetic and extremely large French riggers clambered up to the cockpit and wrenched me out, at first not realising that my harness was still locked – possibly inflicting the only injuries that I suffered: a couple of fractured ribs. My gods were certainly smiling on me that day!

Nick Wiles

At 14.45 on 11 January 1975, Captain Nick Wiles departed from Port Harcourt in Wessex Mk.60 5N-AIR (formerly G-AXXL) on a routine flight to Oloibiri flow station, then onwards to Brass Terminal (AGIP terminal) arriving there at 15.30 local time. The aircraft was owned by Bristow who were contracted by Shell Petroleum Development Company Nigeria Ltd. But his return was anything but routine, as Nick recalls:

On descending through approximately 80–90ft on final approach in a nose-high attitude in order to flare slightly to reduce speed, there was a sudden violent vibration. It was so violent that it was more of a hurtling around sensation as I could not see anything at all. All I thought of doing was to get down as soon as possible, so I dumped the collective lever.

The aircraft hit the ground heavily and after some more thrashing around my vision finally returned when all became quiet. The cockpit was filled with what I thought was smoke but transpired to be unburnt fuel fumes and French chalk dust from the starboard float canister which had inflated. Assuming that with such an impact there was likely to be a fire I automatically proceeded to perform the various post-crash vital actions: HP fuel cocks closed, battery

master switch off, etc. Unbeknown to me, these actions had already been done automatically by the 4.5G inertia crash switches. I then exited the aircraft through the right-hand seat window but had no idea that the aircraft was lying on its port side as the port undercarriage had collapsed.

According to an eye witness – a supply boat skipper who was on the bridge of his vessel alongside the terminal nearby – I leaped out from the cockpit in one bound and ran. Once I was about 50yd away I looked back at the aircraft which to my surprise was actually not on fire. It then occurred to me that I had better go back for the one passenger who, worryingly, had not appeared!

With the aircraft on its side, I found it difficult to climb up the underbelly as there were no hand or foot holds – why would there be – and the surface was oily. But eventually I succeeded to clamber up and slid open the cabin door.

TOP Wessex Mk.60 G-AWOX prior to the accident. *(Author's collection)*

ABOVE The shattered remains of G-AWOX. *(Tony Stafford)*

The passenger had been sitting almost directly under my seat on the starboard side and was now held suspended by his seatbelt. I reached down and released his belt and then hauled him out before telling him to run.

By the time that I was clear again from the aircraft, the fire engine had arrived and had commenced spraying the Wessex with fire-retardant foam. I could see that the whole tail boom section from the rear of the cabin had separated and was lying on the ground slightly ahead of the main aircraft. Also, the nose with sand filter assembly had become loose.

The next day the crash site was visited by none other than the Bristow Operations Director himself, Alastair Gordon, and the Finance Manager, Brian Collins, who happened to be visiting Nigeria at the time. Alastair and I had discussed the accident over dinner the night before when he asked me if I thought it possible that a main rotor blade might have failed. I said that the vibration was consistent with that kind of catastrophic event but had no idea really.

When we arrived at the crash site we walked back up the final approach path over a flat, sandy area to the helipad. Sure enough, about 100yd back was the outer half of a main rotor blade lying in the sand virtually undamaged except for the slightly crumpled tip where it fell. The outer blade section was about 13ft long and one could clearly see the striations and crack on the main spar 'D' section. The blade had failed at approximately the mid-point just at the time the translational lift was lost at about 20–25kt.

The blade section and the corresponding inner section were sent to the Air Accidents Investigation Branch (AAIB) at Farnborough for further investigation. The subsequent report noted that the failure was not due to the fact that I was landing as the main disc was offloaded and not under stress. The propagation of the crack in the main spar, the AAIB stated, developed quickly and could have occurred at any time during the flight. Most of my transit had taken place at 1,500–2,000ft over primary rainforest; should the failure have happened a minute or two earlier, the wreckage would have been scattered over a huge area and it is likely that the cause would never have been known.

My position in the cockpit was just about 18in ahead of the main rotor shaft. This accounts for the whiplash – which, along with some bruising from the full harness, was my only physical injury – when flying a machine with only three and a half blades. The passenger fared better than me as he was seated almost directly under the main gearbox. The severe out-of-balance forces were enough to cause the whole tail section to detach and the nose door to almost separate. The tail coming off in flight was what the supply boat skipper thought had caused the accident.

There was understandably much interest in the accident at the time, not least because the Queen's Flight also operated the Wessex and they had a policy of changing all components at half-life. To my knowledge this blade had failed at slightly less than 750 hours which I believe was half-life (full life being 1,500 hours).

I owe my life, and that of the passenger, to the strength of the main fuselage section of the Wessex. Despite minor injuries and suffering some delayed shock, I was back flying the mighty Wessex again just over a week later.

Appendix

Wessex HAS Mk.1 operating units

- 700H Naval Air Squadron, RNAS Culdrose
- 706 Naval Air Squadron, RNAS Culdrose
- 737 Naval Air Squadron, RNAS Portland
- 771 Naval Air Squadron, RNAS Portland
- 814 Naval Air Squadron, RNAS Culdrose
- 815 Naval Air Squadron, RNAS Culdrose
- 819 Naval Air Squadron, RAF Ballykelly
- 826 Naval Air Squadron, RNAS Culdrose
- 829 Naval Air Squadron, RNAS Culdrose

Wessex HC Mk.2 operating units

- 2 Flying Training School, RAF Shawbury
- 22 Squadron, RAF Finningley; RAF Boulmer; RAF Chivenor ('A' Flight); RAF Leuchars ('B' Flight); RAF Valley ('C' Flight); RAF Manston ('E' Flight); RAF Coltishall ('F' Flight)
- 18 Squadron, RAF Gütersloh, RAF Odiham, RAF Aldergrove, RAF Acklington, RAF Nicosia, RAF Wildenrath
- 28 (Army Co-operation) Squadron, RAF Kai Tak and RAF Sek Kong, Hong Kong
- 32 (The Royal) Squadron, RAF Northolt
- 60 Squadron, RAF Benson
- 72 Squadron, RAF Odiham, RAF Gütersloh, RAF Aldergrove and RAF Nicosia
- 84 Squadron, RAF Akrotiri
- 103 Squadron, Tengah
- 240 Operational Conversion Unit, RAF Odiham
- HOC Flight, RAF Odiham
- Search and Rescue Training Unit (SARTU), RAF Valley

Wessex HAS Mk.3 operating units

- 700H Naval Air Squadron, RNAS Culdrose and RNAS Portland
- 706 Naval Air Squadron, RNAS Culdrose
- 737 Naval Air Squadron, RNAS Portland
- 814 Naval Air Squadron, RNAS Culdrose
- 819 Naval Air Squadron, RAF Ballykelly
- 820 Naval Air Squadron, RNAS Culdrose
- 826 Naval Air Squadron, RNAS Culdrose

RIGHT Wessex HC Mk.2 brochure. *(Leonardo Helicopters)*

Wessex HCC Mk.4 operating units

- The Queen's Flight, RAF Benson

Wessex HU Mk.5 operating units

- 700V Naval Air Squadron, RNAS Culdrose
- 707 Naval Air Squadron, RNAS Culdrose, RNAS Yeovilton
- 771 Naval Air Squadron, RNAS Portland, RNAS Culdrose
- 772 Naval Air Squadron, RNAS Lee-on-Solent, RNAS Portland
- 781 Naval Air Squadron, RNAS Lee-on-Solent
- 845 Naval Air Squadron, RNAS Yeovilton
- 846 Naval Air Squadron, RNAS Yeovilton
- 847 Naval Air Squadron, RNAS Yeovilton, RNAS Sembawang
- 848 Naval Air Squadron, RNAS Yeovilton

Wessex HU Mk.5C operating units

- 84 Squadron, RAF Akrotiri

Wessex Mk.60 Operators

- Bristow Helicopters
- Flight Services International
- Helicopter Hire
- Sykes
- Glosair

Glossary

AAC	Army Air Corps	HOCF	Helicopter Operational Conversion Flight
AAIB	Air Accidents Investigation Branch	HP	High pressure
AC	Alternating current	HQNI	Headquarters Northern Ireland
AES	Air Engineering School	HRH	His/Her Royal Highness
AFCS	Automatic Flight Control System	HT	Helicopter Trainer
ALM	Air Load Master	HU	Helicopter Utility
ANZUK	Australia, New Zealand, United Kingdom	IFF	Identification Friend or Foe
ARB	Air Registration Board	IFTU	Intensive Flying Trials Unit
ARI	Airborne Radio Installation	IGB	Intermediate gearbox
AS	Anti-submarine	IGV	Inlet Guide Vane
ASE	Auto Stabilisation Equipment	IPN	Isopropyl nitrate
ASI	Air speed Indicator	kt	Knots
ASW	Anti-submarine warfare	lb	Pounds (weight)
AVGAS	Aviation gasoline	LP	Low pressure
BHL	Bristow Helicopters Limited	Mk	Mark
BIM	Blade Inspection Method	MoD	Ministry of Defence
BP	British Petroleum	MoS	Ministry of Supply
BS381C	British standard for paint	MRB	Main rotor blade
CAA	Civil Aviation Authority	MRGB	Main rotor gearbox
CASEVAC	Casualty Evacuation	MRH	Main rotor head
CFS	Central Flying School	NAS	Naval Air Squadron
COMR	Civil-Owned Military-Registered	NATO	North Atlantic Treaty Organization
CWP	Centralised Warning Panel	Nr	Main rotor speed
DC	Direct current	NVG	Night vision goggles
DHFS	Defence Helicopter Flying School	OCU	Operational Conversion Unit
DSO	Distinguished Service Order	OM	Oil mineral (heavy-duty engine oil)
EGV	Exit Guide Vane	OX	Synthetic oil
EMRU	Electromagnetic Release Unit	PO	Petty Officer
FAA	Federal Aviation Administration	PPI	Plan Position Indicator
FPT	Free power turbine	PSP	Pierced steel planking
FSII	Fuel system icing inhibitor	Radar	Radio detection and ranging
FTS	Flying Training School	RAF	Royal Air Force
GPMG	General-purpose machine gun	RAN	Royal Australian Navy
GPS	Global Positioning System	RFA	Royal Fleet Auxiliary
HAECO	Hong Kong Aircraft Engineering Company	RMP	Royal Military Police
HAR	Helicopter Air Rescue	RN	Royal Navy
HAS	Helicopter anti-submarine	RNAS	Royal Naval Air Station
HC	Helicopter cargo	RNAY	Royal Naval Aircraft Yard
HCC	Helicopter communications	RP	Rocket projectile
HF	High-frequency	rpm	Revolutions per minute
HIFR	Helicopter In-Flight Refuelling	SACRU	Semi-automatic Cargo Release Unit
HMAS	Her Majesty's Australian Ship	SAR	Search and Rescue
HMS	His/Her Majesty's Ship	SARTU	Search and Rescue Training Unit
		SARW	Search and Rescue Wing

SAS	Special Air Service		TRU	Transformer Rectifier Unit
SF	Special Forces		UHF	Ultra-high frequency
SH	Support helicopter		UN	United Nations
SHFDNI	Support Helicopter Force Detachment Northern Ireland		UNFICYP	United Nations Peacekeeping Force In Cyprus
SHFNI	Support Helicopter Force Northern Ireland		USAF	United States Air Force
			USMC	United States Marine Corps
shp	shaft horsepower		USN	United States Navy
Sonar	Sound navigation and ranging		VVIP	Very Very Important Person
SRCU	Short Range Conversion Unit		WOCF	Wessex Operational Conversion Flight
SRT	Short Range Transport			
SSL	Speed select lever		WSF	Wessex Servicing Flight
TRGB	Tail rotor gearbox		WTF	Wessex Training Flight

Bibliography and sources

Ballance, Theo, Howard, Lee and Sturtivant, Ray, *The Squadrons and Units of the Fleet Air Arm*, Air-Britain, 2016

Bristow, Alan with Malone, Patrick, *Alan Bristow – Helicopter Pilot. The Autobiography*, Pen & Sword, 2009

British Aviation Research Group, *Falklands, the Air War*, BARG, 1985

Chartres, John, *Helicopter Rescue*, Ian Allan, 1980

Chartres, John, *Fly for their Lives*, Airlife, 1988

Fay, John, *The Helicopter: History, Piloting & How it Flies*, David & Charles, 1989

Grayson, Jerry, *Rescue Pilot – Cheating the Sea*, Bloomsbury, 2015

Howard, Lee, Burrow, Mick and Myall, Eric, *Fleet Air Arm Helicopters since 1943*, Air-Britain, 2011

Leeming, Geoffrey, *From Borneo to Lockerbie – Memoirs of an RAF Helicopter Pilot*, Pen & Sword, 2013

Manning, Charles: *Fly Navy – The View from the Cockpit 1945–2000*, Leo Cooper, 2000

Postgate, Malcolm R., *Operation Firedog – Air Support in the Malayan Emergency 1948–1960*, HMSO, 1992

Skinner, Brian, *Voices of the Fleet Air Arm during Borneo Confrontation 1962 to 1966*, Fastprint Publishing, 2011

Taylor, Bill, *Royal Air Force Germany since 1945*, Midland Counties, 2003

TNA files
ADM 1/28062
ADM 259/148
AIR 2/18405
AIR 2/18462
AIR 2/18558
AIR 20/12075
18 Sqn: AIR 27/2907, 3258, 3287, 3414, 3415
28 Sqn: AIR 27/3050, 3301, 3302, 3426, 3563
72 Sqn: AIR 27/2940, 3100, 3453, 3454, 3588, 3685
78 Sqn; AIR 27/2952, 3103, 3104
103 Sqn: AIR 27/3352
AVIA 18/3212
AVIA 18/3216
AVIA 54/2311
T 225/1610
T 225/4084

Index